COMPILED AND EDITED BY
Jon Winokur

TRUE
CONFESSIONS

A PLUME BOOK

PLUME
Published by the Penguin Group
Penguin Books USA Inc., 375 Hudson Street,
New York, New York 10014, U.S.A.
Penguin Books Ltd, 27 Wrights Lane, London W8 5TZ, England
Penguin Books Australia Ltd, Ringwood, Victoria, Australia
Penguin Books Canada Ltd, 10 Alcorn Avenue,
Toronto, Ontario, Canada M4V 3B2
Penguin Books (N.Z.) Ltd, 182-190 Wairau Road,
Auckland 10, New Zealand

Penguin Books Ltd, Registered Offices:
Harmondsworth, Middlesex, England

Published by Plume, an imprint of New American Library,
a division of Penguin Books USA Inc.
Previously published in a Dutton edition.

First Plume Printing, June, 1993
10 9 8 7 6 5 4 3 2 1

Acknowledgments for permission to reprint are listed on page 275.

℗ REGISTERED TRADEMARK—MARCA REGISTRADA

LIBRARY OF CONGRESS CATALOGING-IN-PUBLICATION DATA
True confessions / compiled and edited by Jon Winokur.
ISBN 0-452-27001-4
1. Aphorisms and apothegms.   I. Winokur, Jon.
PN6269.A2T78   1993   92-44549
082—dc20   CIP

Printed in the United States of America
Original hardcover design by Barbara Huntley

INDEX

D

E

Edward VIII, King of England, 25
Eichmann, Adolf, 267
Einstein, Albert, 32, 63, 119, 216, 226, 262
Eisenhower, Dwight D., 12
Ekland, Britt, 256
Eliot, T. S., 245
Elizabeth II, Queen of England, 23, 24, 25
Elizabeth, Queen Mother of England, 30
Ellington, Duke, 136
Ellison, Harlan, 10, 95
Ephron, Nora, 149, 152
Evans, Joni, 159

F

Fassbinder, Rainer Werner, 38
Faulkner, William, 172, 271
Fawcett, Farrah, 212
Feiffer, Jules, 189
Felder, Raoul Lionel, 273
Feldman, Marty, 160
Fellini, Federico, 61, 113
Ferrare, Cristina, 129, 165
Field, Sally, 86, 136
Fields, W. C., 64, 135, 270
Fischer, Bobby, 167

Fisher, Carrie, 12, 13, 41, 82, 96, 152, 222, 263
Flaubert, Gustave, 241
Flynn, Errol, 67, 266
Flynt, Larry, 245
Fonda, Henry, 249
Ford, Gerald, 36, 54, 249
Ford, Harrison, 60
Forster, E. M., 242
Forsyth, Frederick, 181
Forsythe, John, 207
Fosse, Bob, 213
Foster, Jodie, 115, 180
Frayn, Michael, 147
Freud, Sigmund, 241, 250
Frost, Robert, 256, 265, 271
Fuller, R. Buckminster, 63
Fussell, Paul, 41

G

Gable, Clark, 21, 49, 249
Gabor, Eva, 215
Gabor, Zsa Zsa, 70, 123, 211, 242
Gallup, George, 246
Gandhi, Mohandas K., 229–33
Garbo, Greta, 39, 248, 261
García Márquez, Gabriel, 254

About the Author

JON WINOKUR confesses to reading *People* avidly and to watching *Entertainment Tonight* without irony. He is the editor of several books, including the best-selling *The Portable Curmudgeon, Zen to Go*, and *Mondo Canine*. He lives in Pacific Palisades, California.

"Losing my virginity was a career move."
—Madonna

In this ultimate bedside reader for inveterate voyeurs, irredeemable eavesdroppers, and connoisseurs of celebrity revelations, everyone from Prince Charles to Eddie Murphy speaks out on their favorite subject: *moi*. With shameless preening about their immortal accomplishments and torrid confessions about their love affairs, they hold forth with an abandon that will satisfy even the most jaded tabloid addict. Whether it is food for thought you crave or popcorn for the soul, Katharine Hepburn, Mick Jagger, Mae West, Tom Selleck, Stephen King, and scores of other world-class icons will gratify your appetite for outrageously naked truths about their lives. *True Confessions* is essential reading for *People* people, National Enquirers—and all of us who want to know what the famous and infamous see when they look in the mirror.

CONTENTS

*If we weren't all so interested in ourselves,
life would be so uninteresting
we couldn't endure it.*
SCHOPENHAUER

INTRODUCTION

This book is about the private lives of famous people. Through first-person-singular quotations, it charts what they think and what they feel, how they see the world and how they see themselves. It collects revealing statements made by celebrities in profiles and interviews, autobiographies and memoirs, as well as juicy personal disclosures mined from the annals of art, science, business, politics, religion and philosophy.

When I began my research I quickly realized that famous people love to confess their innermost thoughts and emotions. They tell you the sordid truth about their love affairs, they reveal family skeletons, they pour their hearts out about their hopes, their dreams, their fears. They divulge the secrets of their success and brag about their claims to fame. They take stands on the important issues and lament the way things might have been. In short, they tell you everything you ever wanted to know about their private lives, and then some.

Since this is a book of confessions, I'll begin with one of my own: I love this stuff. I'm not sure why. I think there's more to it than mere schadenfreude (though I do take consolation in the knowledge that the rich and famous are miserable too), and it goes beyond the cliché that celebrities are our only royalty (which isn't even true: we have the British royals—see page 23). There seems to be a symbiotic relationship in which the celebrity's compulsion to reveal intimate details fuels the public's obsession with those details. I mean, I'm an avid reader of *People* and *Us*, I watch *Entertainment Tonight* without irony and *A Current Affair* with only mild revulsion, and I still think about the "Rat Pack." There, I feel much better.

Anyone who likes gossip is a potential connoisseur of true confessions. Gossip is secondhand, warmed-over gruel; true confessions are firsthand, deep dish. Now, if that makes you squeamish, if you're reluctant to indulge in such voyeurism, let me assure you that it's okay to revel in celebrity revelations. It may not have any redeeming social value, but unlike a growing list of retrograde pleasures, there are no harmful side effects. If you don't inhale.

J.W.
Pacific Palisades, California
1992

I was born at the age of twelve on the Metro-Goldwyn-Mayer lot. JUDY GARLAND

When I was born, I owed twelve dollars. GEORGE S. KAUFMAN

I was born in a balcony at the Lawndale Theater on Roosevelt Road near Pulaski in Chicago. My daddy owned the picture show. ALICE KAHN

I was born Beatrice Gladys Lillie at an extremely tender age because my mother needed a fourth at meals. BEATRICE LILLIE

To my embarrassment, I was born in bed with a lady. WILSON MIZNER

I was caesarean born. You can't really tell, although whenever I leave a house, I go out through a window. STEVEN WRIGHT

I Am Born—1

When I was born, I was so surprised I couldn't talk for a year and a half. GRACIE ALLEN

I was born in 1896 and my parents were married in 1919.   J. R. ACKERLEY

I was born in 1939. The other big event of that year was the outbreak of the Second World War, but for the moment that did not affect me.   CLIVE JAMES

I was born for soccer, just as Beethoven was born for music.   PÉLÉ

I was born in Alabama, but I only lived there for a month before I'd done everything there was to do.   PAULA POUNDSTONE

I was born on a storm-swept rock and hate the soft growth of sun-baked lands where there is no frost in men's bones.   LIAM O'FLAHERTY

I was born in Tampico, Illinois, in a little flat above the bank building. We didn't have any other contact with the bank than that.
                              RONALD REAGAN

I was born because it was a habit in those days. People didn't know any different.
                              WILL ROGERS

Parentage,
Childhood
and Family
Life

My ancestors were Puritans from England. They arrived here in 1648 in the hope of finding greater restrictions than were permissible under English law at that time.

GARRISON KEILLOR

My ancestors wandered lost in the wilderness for forty years because even in biblical times, men would not stop to ask for directions.

ELAYNE BOOSLER

I was brought up in a clergyman's household, so I am a first-class liar.

DAME SYBIL THORNDIKE

I don't know who my grandfather was; I am much more concerned to know what his grandson will be.　ABRAHAM LINCOLN

My grandmother was a very tough woman. She buried three husbands. Two of them were just napping.　RITA RUDNER

My grandfather was a Jewish juggler: he used
to worry about six things at once.

RICHARD LEWIS

I ... was born to confusion and totally im-
mersed in it for several years, owning three
different names until the age of fourteen and
living in about thirty different hotels, lodgings
and flats, each of which was hailed as "home"
until such time as my mother and I flitted,
leaving behind, like a paper-chase, a wake of
unpaid bills.

ALEC GUINNESS

I remember seeing [my mother] kiss Rex Reed.
He was her client and she treated him like a
son. She treated me like a client.

BUDD SCHULBERG

My dad was the town drunk. Usually that's
not so bad, but New York City?

HENNY YOUNGMAN

I came from a bunch of Irish drunks, my
mother and father. They had half a bag on
most of the time.

MARLON BRANDO

I am a Harp, that is my history, Irish and Catholic, from steerage to suburbia in three
generations.

JOHN GREGORY DUNNE

My mother is Irish, my father is black and Venezuelan, and me—I'm tan, I guess.

MARIAH CAREY

I came from a family where gravy was a beverage and ketchup was a vegetable.

ERMA BOMBECK

As a child my family's menu consisted of two choices: take it or leave it.   BUDDY HACKETT

We never talked, my family. We communicated by putting Ann Landers articles on the refrigerator.   JUDY GOLD

The only thing I ever said to my parents when I was a teenager was "Hang up, I got it!"

CAROL LEIFER

My parents taught me their work ethic, which included always working hard, not getting into trouble with the law, and appearances are what people think you're about. Therefore, no earring.   JIMMY SMITS

Of course, the last thing my parents wanted was a son who wears a cocktail dress that glitters, but they've come around to it.   DIVINE

My parents forced me to take accordion lessons when I was a toddler.   JUDY TENUTA

My father invented a cure for which there was no disease, and unfortunately my mother caught it and died of it.   VICTOR BORGE

I can't remember my father at all. I can remember my mother only through a child's eyes. I don't know which fact is the sadder.
CLIVE JAMES

When I was six years old my mother told me I was a genius.   NICOLAS SLONIMSKY

I was a twerp if ever there was one.
LAURENCE OLIVIER

When I was a kid in the Midwest I got straight A's in school, and I spent thirteen years on the psychiatrist's couch paying for it.
WALLY COX

I never played basketball. I was a geek.
BOB SAGET

I was a real geek when I was a kid. When I was fourteen I looked like a fetus with shoes.
DANA CARVEY

I was a very self-conscious teenager—chubby, one hundred forty pounds, chipmunk cheeks. I still harbor some of those hangups.

CHRISTIE BRINKLEY

No one ever called me pretty when I was a little girl.   MARILYN MONROE

I never thought I was pretty as a child, and that is an awareness I have brought to my roles.   JANE ALEXANDER

I was the nasty one that sat in the toilets and smoked—and made the other girls cry.

TRACEY ULLMAN

I have an elbow that bends the wrong way, and [when I was a teenager] I'd do things like stand in an elevator and the doors would close, and I'd pretend that my arm had got caught in it, and then I'd scream, "Ow, ow, put it back!"   GEENA DAVIS

I know I was cruel to other children because I remember stuffing their nostrils with putty, and beating little boys with stinging nettles.   VITA SACKVILLE-WEST

I never smoked a cigarette until I was nine.   H. L. MENCKEN

It was no great tragedy being Judy Garland's daughter. I had tremendously interesting childhood years—except they had little to do with being a child. LIZA MINNELLI

You really grow up fast in a nightclub. WAYNE NEWTON

I sucked in chisels and hammers with my nurse's milk. MICHELANGELO BUONARROTI

My first recollection is that of a bugle call. GENERAL DOUGLAS MACARTHUR

I went straight from shenanigans to crimes against humanity. GEORGE CARLIN

I was the seventh of nine children. When you come from that far down you have to struggle to survive. ROBERT KENNEDY

Disease, insanity and death were the angels which attended my cradle, and since then have followed me throughout life. I learned early about the misery and dangers of life, and about the afterlife, about the eternal punishment which awaited the children of sin in Hell. EDVARD MUNCH

I was the green monkey, the pariah. And I had no friends. Not just a few friends, or one good friend, or grudging acceptance by other misfits and outcasts. I was alone. All stinking alone, without even an imaginary playmate.

HARLAN ELLISON

I was a loner as a child. I had an imaginary friend—I didn't bother with him.

GEORGE CARLIN

When I was a girl I only had two friends, and they were imaginary. And they would only play with each other.   RITA RUDNER

My sister and I never engaged in sibling rivalry. Our parents weren't that crazy about either one of us.   ERMA BOMBECK

The highlight of my childhood was making my brother laugh so hard that food came out of his nose.   GARRISON KEILLOR

The kindest thing I can say about my childhood is that I survived it.

RUBIN "HURRICANE" CARTER

When I was a boy at school I never minded the lessons. I just resented having to work terribly hard at playing.   JOHN MORTIMER

I went to school in Hooks, Texas, where most
people can't even read the name stitched over
their own pocket.   JOE BOB BRIGGS

The girls [in high school] were big and ugly
and fat and mean. They used to throw french
fries at me.   SEAN YOUNG

It wasn't that no one asked me to the prom, it
was that no one would tell me where it
was.   RITA RUDNER

My childhood was a period of waiting for the
moment when I could send everyone and everything connected with it to hell.
                                   IGOR STRAVINSKY

We didn't have a lot of mirrors when I was
growing up. We had one mirror, a cracked mirror. You know, in my mind's eye I'm beautiful
and tall and thin and glamorous.
                                   BETTE MIDLER

When I remember my family, I always remember their backs. They were always indignantly
leaving places.   JOHN CHEEVER

We were poor when I was young, but the difference then was the government didn't come
around telling you you were poor.
                                   RONALD REAGAN

Parentage, Childhood and Family Life—11

I found out later that we were very poor, but the glory of America is that we didn't know it then. DWIGHT D. EISENHOWER

My childhood is so far away . . . it's like I don't even remember being a child. I think it was someone else who was a child. BOB DYLAN

Till I was thirteen, I thought my name was "Shut Up." JOE NAMATH

I was kind of a mama's boy until I was twenty-one. WOODY HARRELSON

I was street-smart—but unfortunately the street was Rodeo Drive. CARRIE FISHER

When I was a boy, my family took great care with our snapshots. We really planned them. We made compositions. We posed in front of expensive cars, homes that weren't ours. We borrowed dogs. Almost every family picture taken of us when I was young had a different borrowed dog in it. RICHARD AVEDON

I was raised in the Jewish tradition, taught never to marry a Gentile woman, shave on Saturday and, most especially, never to shave a Gentile woman on Saturday. WOODY ALLEN

I come from a big family. As a matter of fact, I never got to sleep alone until I was married.

LEWIS GRIZZARD

I'm not ashamed of my bare-bottomed beginnings.

SOPHIA LOREN

Our family didn't exactly come from the wrong side of the tracks, but we were certainly always within the sound of the train whistles.

RONALD REAGAN

My mom had the breakdown for the family, and I went into therapy for all of us.

CARRIE FISHER

INGMAR BERGMAN
I Remember Mama

Today, as I lean over photographs of my childhood to study my mother's face through a magnifying glass, I try to penetrate long vanished emotions. Yes, I loved her and she is very attractive in the photograph, with her thick center-parted hair above a broad forehead, her soft oval face, gentle sensual mouth, her warm unaffected gaze below dark shapely eyebrows, her small strong hands.

My four-year-old heart was consumed with doglike devotion.

Nevertheless, our relationship was not uncomplicated. My devotion disturbed and irritated her. My expressions of tenderness and my violent outbursts worried her. She often sent me away with cool ironic words and I wept with rage and disappointment. Her relationship with my brother was simpler, for she was always defending him against Father, who brought him up with rigorous sternness in which brutal flogging was a recurrent argument.

I slowly realized that my adoration, alternately gentle and furious, had little effect, so I soon started to test out behavior that would please her and arouse her interest. Illness immediately attracted her sympathy. As I was a sickly child with endless ailments, this did indeed become a painful but successful route to her tenderness. On the other hand, as Mother was a trained nurse, shamming was swiftly seen through and punished in public.

Another way to gain her attention proved more harmful. I learned that Mother could not bear indifference and preoccupation. She used them as *her* weapons. I also learned to subdue my passions, and started on a peculiar game, the primary ingredients of which were arrogance and a cool friendliness. I can remember nothing about what I did, but love makes one enterprising and I quickly succeeded in creating interest in my combination of sensitivity and self-esteem.

My greatest problem was simply that I was never given the opportunity to reveal my game, throw off the mask and allow myself to be enveloped in a love that was reciprocated.

Many years later, when Mother was in the hospital with a tube in her nose after her second heart attack, we talked about our lives. I told her about my sufferings in childhood and she admitted she had been distressed by them, but not in the way I had thought. She had taken her troubles to a famous pediatrician, and he had warned her in solemn terms to reject firmly what he called my "sickly approaches." Every indulgence would damage me for life.

I have a clear memory of a visit to this child specialist. I had refused to go to school, although I was already more than six. Day after day I was dragged or carried, screaming with anguish, into the classroom. I vomited over everything I saw, fainted and lost my sense of balance. In the end, I won the day and school was postponed, but the visit to this famous pediatrician was unavoidable.

He had a large beard, a high collar and smelled of cigars. He pulled down my trousers, seized my insignificant organ in one hand and with the forefinger of his other hand drew a triangle around my crotch, then said to my mother, sitting behind me in her fur-edged coat and dark green velvet hat with a veil, "The boy still looks like a child *here*."

When we got back from the doctor's, I was dressed in my faded yellow smock with its red border and a cat embroidered on the pocket. I was given hot chocolate and cheese sandwiches. Then I went into the nursery, now recaptured from the baby. My brother had scarlet fever and was elsewhere. (Naturally I hoped he would die. The disease was dangerous in those days.) Out of the toy cupboard I took a wooden cart with red wheels and yellow spokes and harnessed a wooden horse to the shafts. The threat of school had faded into a pleasing memory of a success.

Although no one believes me, I have always been a country girl, and still have a country girl's values.   AVA GARDNER

Nobody really knows me: I'm a mixture of self-confidence and insincerity. One thing's for sure—I hate talking about myself.
BARBRA STREISAND

No one really knows me here [in Hollywood]. . . . I paint, write poetry and have a rose garden.   RICHARD GRIECO

My whole career has been devoted to keeping people from knowing me.   LON CHANEY

I'm a very physical person. People don't credit me with much of a brain, so why should I disillusion them?   SYLVESTER STALLONE

I have had my different husbands, my families.
I am fond of them all and I visit them all. But
deep inside me there is the feeling that I belong to show business.   INGRID BERGMAN

> I have this kind of mild, nice-guy exterior, but
> inside, my heart is like a steel trap. I'm really
> quite robotic.   DAN ACKROYD

I am terribly shy, but of course no one believes
me.   CAROL CHANNING

> I became an actor by accident; I'm a business-
> man by design.   JAMES GARNER

I'm actually a thin, serious person but I play
fat and funny, but only for the movies.
DOM DeLUISE

> I called myself king of comedy, but I was a
> harassed monarch. I worked most of the time.
> It was only in the evenings that I laughed.
> MACK SENNETT

I don't pretend to be an ordinary housewife.   ELIZABETH TAYLOR

> If I took my sunglasses off, everyone could see
> that I was lying through my teeth.
> GEORGE MICHAEL

If you want to know all about Andy Warhol,
just look at the surface of my paintings and
films and me, and there I am. There's nothing
behind it.   ANDY WARHOL

> The nicest part is that there are no theatrics. I
> sit at the piano and play my songs. That is
> what I am.   NEIL SEDAKA

What you choose to do has to do with who
you are. If you saw my work and you met me,
you wouldn't be shocked.   JACK NICHOLSON

> Just because I've got spiked hair doesn't mean
> I'm not a loving, passionate person.
>   BILLY IDOL

I can do something else besides stuff a ball
through a hoop. My biggest resource is my
mind.   KAREEM ABDUL-JABBAR

> I have bursts of being a lady, but it doesn't last
> long.   SHELLEY WINTERS

I'm still the little southern girl from the wrong
side of the tracks who really didn't feel like
she belonged.   FAYE DUNAWAY

Look, I vacuum. And I've cleaned toilet bowls in my life. I clean the bowls with a brush. I wasn't born with any silver spoon.   LEONA HELMSLEY

They told me to fix my teeth, change my nose, even get out of the business. But I stayed and learned and didn't give up.   LAUREN HUTTON

I arrived in Hollywood without having my nose fixed, my teeth capped, or my name changed. That is very gratifying to me.
BARBRA STREISAND

In my early days I was a sepia Hedy Lamarr. Now I'm black and a woman, singing my own way.   LENA HORNE

I'm like a wild animal who's behind bars. I need air. I need space.   KLAUS KINSKI

I am a sensitive writer, actor, and director. Talking business disgusts me. If you want to talk business, call my disgusting personal manager.   SYLVESTER STALLONE

This king stuff is pure bull. I eat and drink and go to the bathroom just like anybody else. I'm just a lucky slob from Ohio who happened to be in the right place at the right time.
CLARK GABLE

I'm a loner. I like a good meal, a good script, and a good BM.   JACK KLUGMAN

I am just a simple doctor. All I wanted to do
. . . was to found a small hospital.
ALBERT SCHWEITZER

Music sometimes brings tears to my eyes . . .
I'm not ashamed to admit it.
BENITO MUSSOLINI

I was Miss Congeniality in the Miss Teenage
America Pageant. I don't tell that to many people—I've always felt that was so embarrassing.
But really—that's really who I am. That's
me. CYBILL SHEPHERD

I'm not a sexy person in real life.
TINA TURNER

I'm just a nice, clean-cut Mongolian boy.
YUL BRYNNER

I'm really a pussycat—with an iron tail.
RONA BARRETT

I just wanted to be an ordinary parish
priest. MARTIN SCORSESE

I'm an introvert. I don't want to be famous.
GEORGE LUCAS

I'm an introvert in an extrovert's profession. RICHARD NIXON

THE WINDSORS
The Royal Family, Ltd.

We're not a family, we're a firm.   GEORGE VI

They say an Englishman's home is his castle.
What I want is to turn my castle into a
home.   QUEEN ELIZABETH

We live in what virtually amounts to a museum, which docs not happen to a lot of
people.   PRINCE PHILIP

Life in Buckingham Palace isn't too bad, but
too many formal dinners. Yuk!
                          PRINCESS DIANA

Living in Buckingham Palace is like living
over the shop.   PRINCE PHILIP

I'm no angel, but I'm no Bo-Peep either.
                          PRINCESS MARGARET

I'm the first queen who's ever been able to
drive.   QUEEN ELIZABETH

[I'm an] uncultured, polo-playing clot.

PRINCE PHILIP

Brain the size of a pea, I've got.

PRINCESS DIANA

[I'm a] discredited Balkan prince of no particular merit or distinction.   PRINCE PHILIP

The absurd thing about being a duke or a prince is that you are a professional ignoramus.   DUKE OF GLOUCESTER

I don't enjoy my public obligations. I was not made to cut ribbons and kiss babies.

PRINCESS MICHAEL

I have as much privacy as a goldfish in a bowl.   PRINCESS MARGARET

I'm one of the most governed people you could hope to meet—almost permanently under arrest.   PRINCE PHILIP

If someone is going to shoot you, there is nothing much you can do about it. If you're going to start worrying about it, it's time to give up.   PRINCE CHARLES

If someone wants to get me, it is too easy.

QUEEN ELIZABETH

Every time I lend my lighter, somebody pinches it. PRINCESS MARGARET

Constitutionally I don't exist. PRINCE PHILIP

I love looking at houses, but I never get the chance. It would be too awkward to invite myself in. My husband heard me talking about this one day and ever since then, if we are in the car and pass by a nice house, he drives up to it to have a look. I get terribly embarrassed sometimes, and all I can do is duck down and hide. QUEEN ELIZABETH

Frankly, I don't like to see a play from the Royal Box. I'd far sooner sit where I can see the front only. I don't want to be peering into the wings to see who's coming on next. GEORGE VI

I don't like to be "Highnessed." Just call me "Sir." PRINCE PHILIP

One can't really dance in a tiara. QUEEN ELIZABETH

I have found it impossible to carry the heavy burden of responsibility and to discharge my duties as king as I would wish to do without the help and support of the woman I love. EDWARD VIII

When I appear in public people expect me to neigh, grind my teeth, paw the ground and swish my tail—none of which is easy.

PRINCESS ANNE

I sometimes wonder if two thirds of the globe is covered in red carpet.   PRINCE CHARLES

I never see any home cooking. All I get is fancy stuff.   PRINCE PHILIP

The trouble with being a princess is that it is so hard to have a pee.   PRINCESS DIANA

There are people who wait around for the moment when you pick your nose to take a photograph of you.   PRINCE PHILIP

I simply treat the press as though they were children.   PRINCE CHARLES

The only time I worry [about the press] is when I'm up at Balmoral fishing. When I'm standing in the river for hours I sometimes have a pee in the water. And I'm always petrified some cameraman is going to catch me at it.   PRINCE CHARLES

My family always cringes when they hear the sound of a motor drive.   PRINCE ANDREW

THE WINDSOR FAMILY TREE

Perhaps the thing I might do best is to be a
long-distance lorry driver.   PRINCESS ANNE

I would like to be the head of an advertising
agency.   DUCHESS OF WINDSOR

I have no ambition. Isn't that terrible?
                            PRINCESS MARGARET

I'd like to get my conk fixed. It's too big.
                              PRINCESS DIANA

I just want to be normal.   PRINCE CHARLES

I doubt I've achieved anything likely to be
remembered.   PRINCE PHILIP

It's simple. I don't eat.
                    PRINCESS MARGARET, on how
                    she loses weight

I'd walk a mile for a bacon sandwich.
                              PRINCESS DIANA

I just come and talk to the plants, really—very
important to talk to them, they respond I
find.   PRINCE CHARLES

I am interested in leisure the way that a poor
man is interested in money. I can't get enough
of it.   PRINCE PHILIP

I love tattoos—especially ones full of color and detail.   PRINCESS DIANA

Dentopedology is the science of opening your mouth and putting your foot in it. I've been practicing it for years.   PRINCE PHILIP

My father was frightened of his mother, I was frightened of my father, and I am damned well going to see to it that my children are frightened of me.   GEORGE V

I am often asked whether it is because of some genetic trait that I stand with my hands behind, like my father. The answer is that we both have the same tailor. He makes our sleeves so tight that we can't get our hands in front.   PRINCE CHARLES

[My childhood was] not necessarily particularly unhappy.   PRINCE PHILIP

I learned the way a monkey learns—by watching its parents.   PRINCE CHARLES

I don't remember any love affairs. One must keep love affairs quiet.   DUCHESS OF WINDSOR

I don't actually like children.   PRINCESS ANNE

I sometimes feel like shooting the queen's corgis.
PRINCESS MICHAEL

I wish I had been born Bob Geldof.
PRINCE CHARLES

I'm not as nice as you think I am.
THE QUEEN MOTHER

I am not one of those people who would rather act than eat. Quite the reverse. My own desire as a boy was to retire. That ambition has never changed. GEORGE SANDERS

When I was a child, what I wanted to be when I grew up was an invalid. QUENTIN CRISP

I have known exactly what I wanted since I was eight years old. My husband chased me until I caught him. PIA ZADORA

When I started out, I didn't have any desire to be an actress or to learn how to act. I just wanted to be famous. KATHARINE HEPBURN

It's been my dream [to play Lolita] since I was five. DREW BARRYMORE

My goal is to find the strength to stop acting. GIANCARLO GIANNINI

Most actors want to play Othello, but all I've really wanted to play is Chance the gardener.
                                                    PETER SELLERS

My main goal is to tell a story.
                                                    STEPHEN SONDHEIM

Mood is what I am after. ANDREW WYETH

I hope I die before I get old.
                                                    PETE TOWNSHEND

I want to go on until they have to shoot me.
                                                    BARBARA STANWYCK

When I die I want to decompose in a barrel of porter and have it served in all the pubs in Dublin.
                                                    J. P. DONLEAVY

Everybody wants to be Cary Grant. Even I want to be Cary Grant.
                                                    CARY GRANT

I want to understand the universe, how it came into being. Otherwise, life just seems pointless.
                                                    STEPHEN HAWKING

I want to know how God created the world. I am not interested in this or that phenomenon, in the spectrum of this or that element; I want to know his thoughts; the rest are details.
                                                    ALBERT EINSTEIN

I like things big. When I die, I want a huge casket that I can roll around in and dial 9 to get out from. ARSENIO HALL

Someday I want to be rich. Some people get so rich they lose all respect for humanity. That's how rich I want to be.   RITA RUDNER

I'd like to be rich enough so I could throw soap away after the letters are worn off.
ANDY ROONEY

I want to live like Marie Antoinette, and I'm going to.   JOAN RIVERS

I've always wanted to grow up to be Alice Roosevelt Longworth.   PAUL MONETTE

If I had not been born Perón, I would have liked to be Perón.   JUAN PERÓN

I should like one of these days to be so well known, so popular, so celebrated, so famous, that it would permit me . . . to break wind in society, and society would think it a most natural thing.   HONORÉ DE BALZAC

I'd like to be in public office. Hey, I'll never lie, I'll always tell you the truth, and I'll work really hard, which is more than I can say for almost every public official that I know.
CHER

All this time I've just wanted to be blond, beautiful, and five feet, two inches tall.

BEA ARTHUR

In my next life, I'd like to come back five foot, two inches, with the best ass and tits you've ever seen.

ANDIE MACDOWELL

When I started making films, I wanted to make Frank Capra pictures. But I've never been able to make anything but these crazy, tough pictures. You are what you are.

JOHN CASSAVETES

I want to lead a quiet, pseudo-intellectual life and go out and direct a picture two times a year.

BURT REYNOLDS

My ultimate goal is to become a saint.

MARISA BERENSON

Actors often behave like children and so we're taken for children. I want to be grown up.

JEREMY IRONS

I want to be an actress, not a personality.

JILL CLAYBURGH

I had no real ambition about acting, but I knew there had to be something better than the bloody chemist's shop.

GLENDA JACKSON

Someday I'd like a part where I can lean my elbow against a mantelpiece and have a cocktail.   CHARLES BRONSON

I had always wanted to go to war. I wanted to write a book. It was something I had to do.
          MICHAEL HERR

I've had a lifelong ambition to be a professional baseball player, but nobody would sign me.   GERALD FORD

I'm the Jackie Robinson era. I wanted to play second base, wear 42 on my back.
          ARTHUR ASHE

I always wanted to go into politics, but I was never light enough to get on the team.
          ART BUCHWALD

I started out to be a sex fiend, but I couldn't pass the physical.   ROBERT MITCHUM

I would like to be a beautiful male prostitute—with a sting in my bottom.   LORD BYRON

My most fervent wish is that I shall meet a man who loves me for myself and not my money.   CHRISTINA ONASSIS

My lifelong ambition has been to spend my money as soon as I can get it.

EDWARD DMYTRYK

I'd like to have money. And I'd like to be a good writer. These two can come together, and I hope they will, but if that's too adorable, I'd rather have money. DOROTHY PARKER

My sole literary ambition is to write one good novel, then retire to my hut in the desert, assume the lotus position, compose my mind and senses, and sink into meditation, contemplating my novel. EDWARD ABBEY

I'd like to live like a poor man with lots of money. PABLO PICASSO

I want to make Art. FRANK CAPRA

My dream is to save women from nature.

CHRISTIAN DIOR

It's always been my dream to own a bar.

RON NESSEN

I would like to play for audiences who are not using my music to stimulate their sex organs. ORNETTE COLEMAN

I'd like to autograph someone's face.

SID VICIOUS

I've always wanted to throw an egg into an electric fan.   OLIVER HERFORD

I know my films upset people. I *want* to upset people.   KEN RUSSELL

I want to build a house with my films. Some of them are the cellar, some are the walls, and some are the windows. But I hope in the end there will be a house.

RAINER WERNER FASSBINDER

I want to make *The Grace Metalious Story*. She wrote *Peyton Place*, became rich, bought Cadillacs, and killed herself. That's a great American story.   JOHN WATERS

I want to be the girl in *Indiana Jones*. I would love to do an adventure movie where I was saving the world. It might be cool if I used a lot of kitchen tools to fight off the enemy.

ROSEANNE BARR

I want to murder painting.   JOÁN MIRÓ

I don't believe in style; I want to be a machine.   ANDY WARHOL

I like joy; I want to be joyous; I want to have fun on the set; I want to wear beautiful clothes

and look pretty. I want to smile, and I want to
make people laugh. And that's all I want.

> DORIS DAY

> It is an aim of my life to die without having
> written a column about who will win the New
> Hampshire primary. But, then, I may be the
> only journalist who has never been to New
> Hampshire.   GEORGE WILL

I've always wanted two lives: one for the movies, and one for myself.   GRETA GARBO

> I don't want to be normal. Who wants to be
> normal?   DAVID O. SELZNICK

I don't want to be remembered. These are de-
humanizing times. It's best to be forgotten.

> JERZY KOSINSKI

> I hope to God I don't win an Oscar. It would
> really depress me if I did.   DUSTIN HOFFMAN

The last thing I want to be is a rich black su-
perstar. I just want to act.   JAMES EARL JONES

> All I want is the best of everything and there's
> very little of that left.   CECIL BEATON

I'd love to sell out completely. It's just that nobody has been willing to buy.

JOHN WATERS

Everyone knows that people outside show business have show business fantasies—to be an actor, write a script, direct. What most people don't know is that people in show business have retail fantasies—a little restaurant, maybe a ball team. I want a bookstore.

RICHARD DREYFUSS

I'm an old-fashioned guy. I want to have a normal life, I want to get married and have kids. I want to be an old man with a beer belly sitting on a porch, looking at a lake or something.　　　　　　JOHNNY DEPP

I want to be the Shirley MacLaine of porno.　　　　　ANNIE SPRINKLE

I want to be the white man's brother, not his brother-in-law.　　MARTIN LUTHER KING, JR.

I want to have a baby, and I want Peter Jennings to be the father. . . . I know he's married, but we could just have a cheap and tawdry affair.　　　　　　SHEENA EASTON

I've always had a hidden wish, a frustrated desire, to run a hotel.　　EDWARD HEATH

I want everybody in the United States to be very highly educated, to have super taste. I mean, people say, "But aren't you an elitist?" and I say, "Yes, but I want everybody to be an elitist." PAUL FUSSELL

This is really absurd, but my Secret Ambition is to be able, just *once*, to walk into a party and *not* have about seventeen gorgeous women tell me that I look exactly like Kevin Costner, only taller. DAVE BARRY

At my height, I'd like to boss a group of men around. CARRIE FISHER

I wanted to become a work of art myself, and not an artist. BERNARD BERENSON

I wanted to be an art businessman or a business artist. Being good in business is the most fascinating kind of art. ANDY WARHOL

I'm not even sure what I want, but that's not the point—it's that I want it *now*. ELVIS COSTELLO

I have been absolutely hag-ridden with ambition. If I could wish to have anything in the world it would be to be free of ambition. TALLULAH BANKHEAD

me, myself and I

I'm young, I'm fast, I'm pretty, and I can't possibly be beat.
MUHAMMAD ALI

People have misconceptions about me. They thought I was going to end up in a hospital in despair. But I looked twenty years younger. I look like a Greek god.
ED KOCH, former mayor of New York City, after being voted out of office

Yes, I am exactly like the characters in my books. I am very tough and have been known to break a Vienna roll with my bare hands. I am very handsome, have a powerful physique and change my shirt every Monday.
RAYMOND CHANDLER

I don't read books, I write them.
HENRY KISSINGER, asked if he had read a current bestseller

I'm thirty years old, but I read at the thirty-four-year-old level.   DANA CARVEY

When I see myself on the screen, I am so beautiful I jump for joy.   MARIA MONTEZ

I'm an instant star. Just add water and stir.   DAVID BOWIE

They gave me star treatment when I was making a lot of money. But I was just as good when I was poor.   BOB MARLEY

I pride myself on the fact that my work has no socially redeeming value.   JOHN WATERS

I have no use for humility. I am a fellow with an exceptional talent.   JACKIE GLEASON

I have a memory like an elephant. In fact, elephants often consult me.   NOEL COWARD

I have nothing to declare except my genius.
    OSCAR WILDE, to a U.S. Customs
    officer upon his arrival
    in New York

Sometimes I amaze myself. I say this humbly.   DON KING

Most people are not that wonderful. So I thank
God for people like me.   JACKIE MASON

We are all worms. But I do believe that I am
a glow-worm.   WINSTON CHURCHILL

I am not the greatest conductor in this country.
On the other hand, I am better than any
damned foreigner.   SIR THOMAS BEECHAM

I am just too much.   BETTE DAVIS

My problem is intense vanity and narcissism.
I've always had such a good physique and
such intense charm that it's difficult to be true
to myself.   LAWRENCE DURRELL

A lot of people don't like to look at themselves
on the screen. But I've got an ego you can't fit
in this room. So, since I love me so much, I
can tolerate even the worst work.
          DANNY DeVITO

I can hold a note as long as the Chase National
Bank.   ETHEL MERMAN

I've known all my life I could take a bunch of
words and throw them up in the air and they
would come down just right. I'm a semantic
Paganini.   TRUMAN CAPOTE

I'm the most translated writer in the world,
behind Lenin, Tolstoy, Gorki and Jules Verne.
And they're all dead.   MICKEY SPILLANE

I've outdone anyone you can name—Mozart,
Beethoven, Bach, Strauss. Irving Berlin, he
wrote 1,001 tunes. I wrote 5,500.

JAMES BROWN

I am the hero of Africa.   IDI AMIN

I was France.   CHARLES DE GAULLE

I know the Haitian people because I *am* the
Haitian people.

FRANCOIS ("PAPA DOC") DUVALIER

I don't like myself, I'm crazy about myself.

MAE WEST

I'm a highly, highly, highly creative human
being. I write music all of the time, I write
scripts constantly, I run my own production
company. . . . I'm also a very determined busi-
nesswoman. I've got a town to deal with. I've
got a lot of things to do, and I don't have time
to be classified as *difficult*, and I don't have
time to care.   KIM BASINGER

I'm fifty-five, I'm overweight, I'm baldheaded, I'm corny. And I'm on top of the heap.

WILLARD SCOTT

I like to be introduced as America's foremost actor. It saves the necessity of further effort.   JOHN BARRYMORE

All my shows are great. Some of them are bad. But they're all great.   LEW GRADE

People hate me because I am a multifaceted, talented, wealthy, internationally famous genius.   JERRY LEWIS

I have four corporations. You could say I'm a conglomerate.   GARY COLEMAN

Early in life I had a chance to choose between honest arrogance and hypocritical humility. I chose honest arrogance and have seen no occasion to change.   FRANK LLOYD WRIGHT

If I only had a little humility I would be perfect.   TED TURNER

The Secret of My Success

There are two reasons why I'm in show business, and I'm standing on both of them.

BETTY GRABLE

The legs aren't so beautiful, I just know what to do with them. MARLENE DIETRICH

I never go out unless I look like Joan Crawford the movie star. If you want to see the girl next door, go next door. JOAN CRAWFORD

Everything you see, I owe to spaghetti.

SOPHIA LOREN

I owe everything—my success and happiness—to men. DINAH SHORE

I owe nothing to Women's Lib.

MARGARET THATCHER

I am a rebel. I make a picture to please me. If it pleases me, there is a chance it will please others. But it has to please me first.

SAMUEL GOLDWYN

I don't try to guess what a million people will like. It's hard enough to know what I like.

JOHN HUSTON

I have ten commandments. The first nine are, thou shalt not bore. The tenth is, thou shalt have right of final cut. BILLY WILDER

In *Casablanca* there was often nothing in my face. But the audience put into my face what they thought I was giving. INGRID BERGMAN

I think my own desire to be loved is what makes me sexually attractive. DUDLEY MOORE

The only reason they come to see me is that I know life is great—and they know I know it. CLARK GABLE

I came back from the war and ugly heroes were in. ROBERT MITCHUM

I always figured the American public wanted a solemn ass for president, so I went along with them. CALVIN COOLIDGE

I used to tremble from nerves so badly that the only way I could hold my head steady was to lower my chin practically to my chest and look up at Bogie. That was the beginning of The Look.   LAUREN BACALL

Growing up, I drank a lot of milk.
                                    CAL RIPKEN, JR.

Through booze I met two chief justices, fifty world champs, six presidents and DiMaggio and Babe Ruth.   TOOTS SHOR

Tears were to me what glass beads are to African traders.   QUENTIN CRISP

The ideas I stand for are not mine. I borrowed them from Socrates. I swiped them from Chesterfield. I stole them from Jesus. And I put them in a book.   DALE CARNEGIE

People have been telling me stories all my life that I swear they never told anyone else. I must have an open face.   MICHAEL HERR

My talent is a horribly limited one. I want to bless and (more often) I can only giggle. . . . My mind is not very fertile, and any success I might have had is due to my own shrewdness in not doing much.   MAX BEERBOHM

It's not so much that I write well, I just don't write badly very often, and that passes for good on television.　ANDY ROONEY

I have the necessary lack of tact.　TED KOPPEL

I never trust a man unless I've got his pecker in my pocket.　LYNDON BAINES JOHNSON

I am not an animal in my personal life. But in the ring there is an animal inside me. Sometimes it roars when the first bell rings. Sometimes it springs out later in a fight. But I can always feel it there, driving me and pushing me forward. It's what makes me win. It makes me enjoy fighting.　ROBERTO DURAN

Every time I hit it out of the park I was trying to hit it on the ground.　MIKE SCHMIDT

By being so long in the lowest form I gained an immense advantage . . . I got into my bones the essential structure of the normal British sentence—which is a noble thing.
WINSTON CHURCHILL

I am the most spontaneous speaker in the world because every word, every gesture, and every retort has been carefully rehearsed.
GEORGE BERNARD SHAW

Most of what I do came out of the TV theme for *The Cisco Kid*.   CHUCK MANGIONE

It usually takes me more than three weeks to prepare a good impromptu speech.
                                    MARK TWAIN

I've survived because I work cheap and don't take up too much time.   ROBERT MITCHUM

I guess I look so straight and normal nobody expects me to pick my nose and fall.
                                    CHEVY CHASE

It costs a lot of money to look this cheap.
                                    DOLLY PARTON

My quiet exterior used to be a mask for hysteria. After seven years of analysis, it just became a habit.   GENE WILDER

I am the beneficiary of a lucky break in the genetic sweepstakes.   ISAAC ASIMOV

My scare value is high. My arena is controversy. My tough front is my biggest asset.
                                    ROY COHN

I'd hire the devil himself as a writer if he gave me a good story.   SAMUEL GOLDWYN

I paint objects as I think them, not as I see them.
PABLO PICASSO

I do not try to dance better than anyone else. I only try to dance better than myself.
MIKHAIL BARYSHNIKOV

The audience knows I'm not going to do anything after all these years to upset them.
PERRY COMO

It is only air conditioning which makes my architecture tolerable.
PHILIP JOHNSON

I had all the schooling any actress needs. I learned enough to sign contracts.
HERMIONE GINGOLD

When I build something for somebody, I always add $50 million or $60 million onto the price. My guys come in, they say it's going to cost $75 million. I say it's going to cost $125 million. Basically, I did a lousy job. But they think I did a great job.
DONALD TRUMP (in 1984)

I buy when other people are selling.
J. PAUL GETTY

I don't know if I'd have made it without Scientology.
JOHN TRAVOLTA

Claims to Fame

Neil Armstrong was the first man to walk on the moon. I am the first man to piss his pants on the moon. BUZZ ALDRIN

I'm the only person of distinction who's ever had a depression named after him.
HERBERT HOOVER

I am the first Eagle Scout Vice President of the United States! GERALD FORD

I'm the only American alive or dead who presided unhappily over the removal of a vice president and a president.
ALEXANDER M. HAIG, JR.

My one claim to originality among Irishmen is that I never made a speech. GEORGE MOORE

I'm known a little bit for being a nut.

JERRY LEWIS

I wouldn't say I invented tack, but I definitely brought it to its present high popularity.

BETTE MIDLER

I've played more psychotics and freaks and dopers than anyone.

BRUCE DERN

My books always make the best-seller lists in Wolf Hole, Arizona, and Hanksville, Utah.

EDWARD ABBEY

I'm probably the only model in New York who hasn't had breast implants.

KIM ALEXIS

I was the toast of two continents: Greenland and Australia.

DOROTHY PARKER

MADONNA
Our Lady of Perpetual Confession

PART I

My family life at home was very repressive, very Catholic, and I was very unhappy. I was considered the sissy of the family because I relied on feminine wiles to get my way. I wasn't quiet at all. I remember always being told to shut up. I got tape put over my mouth. I got my mouth washed out with soap. Mouthing off comes naturally.

When I [went] to confession, I never told the priest what I thought I'd really done wrong. I'd make up other, smaller crimes. I thought, Look, if I think I've done something wrong, I have a private line to God, and I'll just tell him in my bedroom.

When I was confirmed, I took the name Veronica as my confirmation name because she wiped the face of Jesus. You know, you weren't supposed to help Christ while he was on his way to the Crucifixion; she was not afraid to step out and wipe the sweat off him and help him. So I liked her for doing that, and I took her name.

Sometimes growing up I felt like the unhired help. I was the oldest girl and always got stuck with the main housekeeping chores. I changed so many diapers that I swore I'd never have kids. I felt like I didn't really have a childhood. I was forced to grow up fast. Everybody should have a few years where they are not feeling too responsible, guilty or upset. I really saw myself as a Cinderella with a wicked stepmother.

The idea that the first guy I ever slept with, my lover when I was fifteen, is married and has kids really breaks me up. I wonder if he still loves me. He probably does.

Every once in a while I wake up and go, "My God! I was married once. I was married, and he was the love of my life." It's like a death to deal with.

Sean [Penn] and I had problems. We had this high-visibility life, and that had a lot to do with the demise of the marriage. When you're always being watched, you almost want to kill each other.

When I was married, I did the wash a lot. I liked folding Sean's underwear. I

Growing up, I thought nuns were very beautiful. For several years I wanted to be a nun ... they never wore any makeup and looked really serene. Nuns are sexy.　　　MADONNA

liked mating socks. You know what I love? I love taking the lint out of the lint screen.

I still love Sean and I understand very clearly, now that time has passed, why things didn't work out between us. I miss certain things about our relationship because I really do consider Sean to be my equal—that's why I married him. I don't suppose I've found that yet with anybody else.

I wish I was married and in a situation where having a child would be possible. People say, "Well, have one on your own." I say, "Wait a minute, I'm not interested in raising a cripple. I want a father there. I want someone I can depend on."

I'm dying to meet someone who knows more than me. I keep meeting guys who know less.

How I Do It

I don't use any method. I'm from the let's pretend school of acting.　　HARRISON FORD

My acting technique is to look up at God just before the camera rolls and say, "Give me a break."　　JAMES CAAN

I don't act, I react.　JAMES STEWART

There is a mixture of anarchy and discipline in the way I work.　　ROBERT DE NIRO

I'm not an actress who can create a character. I play me.　　MARY TYLER MOORE

I really don't think about anything until I get on the set.　　VALERIE PERRINE

Paint eyeballs on my eyelids and I'll sleepwalk through any picture.　　ROBERT MITCHUM

I always direct the same film. I can't distinguish one from another.   FEDERICO FELLINI

If my fanny squirms, it's bad. If my fanny doesn't squirm, it's good.   HARRY COHN

When I was in the hair business I produced huge, spectacular shows. Film is just another form of production.   JON PETERS

I bring out the worst in my enemies and that's how I get them to defeat themselves.
ROY COHN

I like stylization. I try to get away with as much as possible until people start laughing at it.   BRIAN DE PALMA

I've never been through psychoanalysis. I solve my problems with the pictures I make.   STEVEN SPIELBERG

I have no desire to prove anything by it. I have never used it as an outlet or as a means of expressing myself. I just dance.
FRED ASTAIRE

God creates, I do not create. I assemble and I steal everywhere to do it—from what I see, from what the dancers can do, from what others do.   GEORGE BALANCHINE

The Mary Hart Leg Cross is a technique, and it's not particularly comfortable. . . . Occasionally I get adventuresome and go so far as to cross the other leg, but it's been left over right for years!   MARY HART

I write music with an exclamation point!
                                    RICHARD WAGNER

I never use a score when conducting an orchestra. Does a lion tamer enter a cage with a book on how to tame a lion?
                                    DIMITRI MITROPOULOS

I try to apply colors like words that shape poems, like notes that shape music.
                                    JOÁN MIRÓ

It [art] grows out of me like my toenails. I have to cut it off and then it grows again.
                                    JEAN ARP

If I like it I say it's mine. If I don't I say it's a fake.   PABLO PICASSO

I try to be as dumb as the camera. It's an immense discipline.   GARY WINOGRAND

I always try to balance the light with the heavy—a few tears for the human spirit in with the sequins and the fringes.

BETTE MIDLER

I base my fashion taste on what doesn't itch.　　　　　　　　　GILDA RADNER

I live by a man's code designed to fit a man's world, yet at the same time I never forget that a woman's first job is to choose the right shade of lipstick.　　　　　　CAROLE LOMBARD

I don't want a lawyer to tell me what I cannot do; I hire him to tell me how to do what I want to do.　　　　　　J. PIERPONT MORGAN

I use the rules to frustrate the law. But I didn't set up the ground rules.　　　　F. LEE BAILEY

I think and think for months and years. Nine-ty-nine times, the conclusion is false. The hun-dredth time I am right.　　　ALBERT EINSTEIN

I just invent, then wait until man comes around to needing what I've invented.

R. BUCKMINSTER FULLER

I never give them hell. I just tell the truth and they think it's hell.　　　HARRY S. TRUMAN

When I want to know what France thinks, I ask myself. CHARLES DE GAULLE

I have a wife and a mistress. From my wife I get love and understanding and sensitivity. From my mistress I get love and passion and sensuality. MARCELLO MASTROIANNI

Anyone who works is a fool. I don't work, I merely inflict myself on the public.
ROBERT MORLEY

I don't make jokes. I just watch the government and report the facts. WILL ROGERS

I make a fortune from criticizing the policy of the government, and then hand it over to the government in taxes to keep it going.
GEORGE BERNARD SHAW

I never write *metropolis* for seven cents because I can get the same price for *city*. I never write *policeman* because I can get the same money for *cop*. MARK TWAIN

I never vote for anyone, I always vote against.
W. C. FIELDS

I have a brain and a uterus, and I use both.
REP. PATRICIA SCHROEDER

I just use my muscles as a conversation piece, like someone walking a cheetah down 42nd Street. ARNOLD SCHWARZENEGGER

I don't invest in anything I don't understand—
it makes more sense to buy TV stations than
oil wells. OPRAH WINFREY

I read a book twice as fast as anybody else.
First I read the beginning, and then I read the
ending, and then I start in the middle and read
toward whichever end I like best.
GRACIE ALLEN

My formula for living is quite simple. I get up
in the morning and I go to bed at night. In
between, I occupy myself as best I can.
CARY GRANT

I never ask myself how I do what I do. After
all, how does it rain? PEARL BAILEY

It isn't what I do, but how I do it. It isn't what
I say, but how I say it. And how I look when
I do it and say it. MAE WEST

Why I Do It

I drink to make other people interesting.
GEORGE JEAN NATHAN

The reason I drink is because when I'm sober
I think I'm Eddie Fisher.   DEAN MARTIN

I write to discover what I think.
DANIEL BOORSTIN

I tape, therefore I am.   STUDS TERKEL

The public seems to want me to dance—and
so I dance.   RAY BOLGER

The public has always expected me to be a
playboy, and a decent chap never lets his public down.   ERROL FLYNN

I'm into pop because I want to get rich, get
famous and get laid.   BOB GELDOF

My lesbianism is an act of Christian charity.
All those women out there are praying for a
man, and I'm giving them my share.

RITA MAE BROWN

I love ice water. . . . I swim all year just to
irritate people. Make them feel weak.

KATHARINE HEPBURN

I walk a lot in New York, not for exercise but
to get from place to place, and because it's the
way of having the least contact with human
beings.

FRAN LEBOWITZ

I have always loved truth so passionately that
I have often resorted to lying as a way of intro-
ducing it into the minds which were ignorant
of its charms.

CASANOVA

I love luxury. And luxury lies not in richness
and ornateness but in the absence of vulgarity.
Vulgarity is the ugliest word in our language.
I stay in the game to fight it.

COCO CHANEL

People want to know why I do this, why I
write such gross stuff. I like to tell them I have
the heart of a small boy—and I keep it in a jar
on my desk.

STEPHEN KING

I don't like to hurt people. I really don't like
it at all. But in order to get a red light at the

intersection, you sometimes have to have an accident.   JACK ANDERSON

I do everything for a reason. Most of the time the reason is money.   SUZY PARKER

I don't write for art's sake. I write for money.   MICKEY SPILLANE

The only reason I'm in Hollywood is that I don't have the moral courage to refuse the money.   MARLON BRANDO

I occasionally play works by contemporary composers ... for two reasons. First to discourage the composer from writing any more and secondly to remind myself how much I appreciate Beethoven.   JASCHA HEIFETZ

I have walked this earth for thirty years and, out of gratitude, want to leave some souvenir.   VINCENT VAN GOGH

My verse represents a handle I can grasp in order not to yield to the centrifugal forces which are trying to throw me off the world.   OGDEN NASH

I go to discos for the same reason I visit bars and hospital emergency rooms. They are all graveyards.   JERZY KOSINSKI

My father refused to have his photograph taken because he, like the Indians, believed that the camera captured your spirit. I don't like having my picture taken because I believe the camera captures your image. ALICE KAHN

> I pretty much try to stay in a constant state of confusion just because of the expression it leaves on my face. JOHNNY DEPP

I'm a publisher because it's a cover for my indulgence. I love to read all day. But I come from nice Puritan stock, and I grew up believing that you have to work all day, so I made reading my work. ANN GETTY

> I don't remember anybody's name. Why do you think the "dahling" thing started? ZSA ZSA GABOR

It's strange how I seem to spend my birthdays away from home. I must subconsciously arrange these trips so the dagger of time pierces an empty bed. JOHN UPDIKE

> I adore not being me. I'm not very good at being me. That's why I adore acting so much. DEBORAH KERR

I can't get the guilties about being an entertainer. I sing for the Lord. NATALIE COLE

Blind Spots

I have tried at various times in my life to grasp the rudiments of such inventions as the telephone, the camera, wireless telegraphy and even the ordinary motorcar, but without success. Television, of course, and radar and atomic energy are so far beyond my comprehension that my brain shudders at the thought of them and scurries for cover like a primitive tribesman confronted for the first time with a Dunhill cigarette lighter. NOEL COWARD

The pencil sharpener is about as far as I have ever got in operating a complicated piece of machinery with any success.
ROBERT BENCHLEY

While edging toward coma during the endless years of baseball this weekend, I suddenly realized I didn't know what a slider was.
RUSSELL BAKER

I have trouble with toast. Toast is very difficult. You have to watch it all the time or it burns up. JULIA CHILD

I only know two tunes. One of them is "Yankee Doodle" and the other isn't.

ULYSSES S. GRANT

I've never seen the point of the sea, except where it meets the land. The shore has point. The sea has none.

ALAN BENNETT

I have a sixth sense, but not the other five. If I wasn't making money, they'd put me away.

RED SKELTON

Actually, I have no regard for money. Aside from its purchasing power, it's completely useless as far as I'm concerned.

ALFRED HITCHCOCK

If you ask me to play myself, I will not know what to do. I do not know who or what I am.

PETER SELLERS

Embarrassing Moments

I put Sugar Ray Robinson on the canvas—
when he tripped over my body.

ROCKY GRAZIANO

Some people instinctively know the stress fac-
tor involved in how much dip a chip can hold.
I never know that. When it breaks, my hand
is thrust into the bowl, and all night I have a
white residue of garlic and sour cream under
my fingernails.   ERMA BOMBECK

When I saw my first screen test I ran from the
projection room screaming.   BETTE DAVIS

The embarrassing thing is that the salad dressing is out-grossing my films.   PAUL NEWMAN

Even when I was a child, I was embarrassed
by Christmas. First of all, it's my birthday. My
mother gave me two shillings to buy a present

for my father, and my father gave me two shillings to buy a present for my mother, and they
both thanked me! I felt a terrible fool.

QUENTIN CRISP

There was this girl in high school I really liked
and finally got the nerve to ask out. So we
went to the movies, and then I took her home.
I thought we'd had a really good time, but she
jumped out of the car and ran into her house.
I didn't understand it until I got home and
looked in the mirror and realized I had gotten
the broccoli from dinner stuck on my teeth. To
this day I can't stand broccoli.

KAREEM ABDUL-JABBAR

When Tom [Cruise] stood up and we shook
hands, I found I was looking down at him. It
was terrifically embarrassing to learn that I
was at least a couple inches taller.

NICOLE KIDMAN

I've had a tough time learning how to act like
a congressman. Today I accidentally spent
some of my own money.

JOSEPH P. KENNEDY II

One night during flight training in the navy, I
had landed my plane without remembering to
put the wheels down. Except for ruining the
propeller, it was a beautiful landing that left

me unscratched. When the plane finally skidded to a stop in showers of sparks, I stood up in the cockpit with spotlights playing over me while sirens screamed and fire trucks and ambulances roared to the scene. Standing there with my stupidity on brightly lit display before the entire squadron, I knew for the first time in my life what utter humiliation felt like.   RUSSELL BAKER

You can imagine my embarrassment when I killed the wrong guy.   JOE VALACHI

KATHARINE HEPBURN
Naked Pictures

Jack and Luddy were looking for trouble. But as far as they got was taking naked pictures. Photographs of me lying on a big sofa which they had in the living room. I posed with total confidence, as I rather fancied myself. I can't remember who else did. . . . They gave me blowups of the pictures. I remember I put them in a straw basket with a straw cover. It had a strap around it. I had it for years. I can't remember when it disappeared. I know that I had it in New York when I first moved there. Then I remember it specifically when I moved into Megs Merrill's apartment at 925 Park Avenue that summer. Megs had married a man named Armitage Watkins called "Wee Willie" Watkins. It seems to me that Willie came to spend the night in the apartment. He opened the straw basket.

"Lots of naked pictures of you," he said.

"Yes," I said.

I think he would have liked me to continue the conversation.

I didn't.

I'm not handsome in the classical sense. The eyes droop, the mouth is crooked, the teeth aren't straight, the voice sounds like a mafioso pallbearer, but somehow it all works.

SYLVESTER STALLONE

I have a face like the behind of an elephant.

CHARLES LAUGHTON

I don't like my face at all. It's always been a great drawback to me.

RALPH RICHARDSON

I have a face that is a cross between two pounds of halibut and an explosion in an old clothes closet. If it isn't mobile, it's dead.

DAVID NIVEN

This mug of mine is as plain as a barn door. Why should people pay thirty-five cents to look at it?

SPENCER TRACY

I have the face of an aging choirboy and the build of an undernourished featherweight. If you can figure out my success on the screen, you're a better man than I.   ALAN LADD

My own mum wouldn't call me pretty.
BOB HOSKINS

I look like a duck. It's the way my mouth sort of curls up, or my nose tilts up. I should have played Howard the Duck.   MICHELLE PFEIFFER

I have reason to believe that I often wear a frown.   J. R. ACKERLEY

I have very big ears. My nickname as a kid was Dumbo.   TED KOPPEL

Under a forehead roughly comparable to that of Javanese and Piltdown man are visible a pair of tiny pig eyes, lit up alternately by greed and concupiscence.   S. J. PERELMAN

My eyes look as though they are peeping over two dirty ping-pong balls.   FRED ALLEN

I went through high school squinting because I was so self-conscious of the size of my eyes.   SUSAN SARANDON

I have eyes like those of a dead pig.

MARLON BRANDO

My feet are dogs.   RUDOLF NUREYEV

My heart is a hamloaf.   RONALD REAGAN

The only parts left of my original body are my elbows.   PHYLLIS DILLER

From the hips up, I'm okay. Until you get to the top of my head, where I have to wear toupees. But then, I've been wearing toupees since the twenties.   GEORGE BURNS

I'm about as tall as a shotgun and just as noisy.   TRUMAN CAPOTE

Even when I was little, I was big.
WILLIAM "THE REFRIGERATOR" PERRY

People think I have an interesting walk. Hell, I'm just trying to hold my gut in.
ROBERT MITCHUM

My breasts are beautiful, and I gotta tell you, they've gotten a lot of attention for what is relatively short screen time.
JAMIE LEE CURTIS

I do have big tits. Always had 'em—pushed 'em up, whacked 'em around. Why not make fun of 'em? I've made a fortune with 'em.

DOLLY PARTON

It would be impossible to be more flat-chested than I am.   CANDICE BERGEN

I am anorexic for an opera singer . . . but I'm a fat anorexic.   KIRI TE KANAWA

My trademarks are a hoarse, grating voice and the face of a retired pugilist: small, narrowed eyes set in puffy features which look as though they might, years ago, have lost on points.

BRODERICK CRAWFORD

I guess I look like a rock quarry that someone has dynamited.   CHARLES BRONSON

I look like somebody's bartender.   DEAN RUSK

I am fifty-four years old, weigh two hundred twenty pounds, and look like the chief dispatcher of a long-distance hauling concern.   JAMES M. CAIN

My photographs do me an injustice. They look just like me.   PHYLLIS DILLER

There are very few people who look like me in this country, and most of them are driving cabs in New York. ERIC BOGOSIAN

In my own mind, I am still a fat brunette from Toledo, and I always will be.

GLORIA STEINEM

I think of my body as a side effect of my mind. Like a thought I had once that manifested it-self—*Oops! Oh no! Manifested. Look at this. Now we have to buy clothes and every-thing.* CARRIE FISHER

I worry about my double chin. I know I'm not a leading man but I still worry.

GENE HACKMAN

They used to photograph Shirley Temple through gauze. They should photograph me through linoleum. TALLULAH BANKHEAD

I like clothes—on other people ... somehow they seem to suffer a sea change when they get on me. They look quite promising in the shop, and not entirely without hope when I get them back into my wardrobe. But then when I put them on, they tend to deteriorate with a very strange rapidity and one feels sorry for them. JOYCE GRENFELL

I haven't got the figure for jeans.

MARGARET THATCHER

Just as a Hollywood pin-up represents sex to dissatisfied erotics, so I represented the ideal daughter millions of fathers and mothers wished they had.   DEANNA DURBIN

I never really thought of myself as a sex symbol—more as a comedienne who could dance.   RITA HAYWORTH

I've always wanted to be a sex symbol, but I don't think I am. I think I'm really hideous and ugly and fluffy and wrinkly and disgusting, so I can't imagine anyone thinking that I was sexually attractive. And if they do, where the fuck are they?   SINEAD O'CONNOR

I've never been in style, so I can't go out of style.   LILLIAN GISH

I'm no actor, and I have sixty-four pictures to prove it.   VICTOR MATURE

I made more lousy pictures than any actor in history.   HUMPHREY BOGART

My movies were the kind they show in prisons and airplanes, because nobody can leave.

BURT REYNOLDS

I started out as a lousy actress and have remained one. BRIGITTE BARDOT

I was the worst actor I ever came across. MICHAEL WILDING

I couldn't act. I had that terrible singing voice, and now I can see I wasn't the greatest tap dancer in the world, either. RUBY KEELER

You could put all the talent I had into your left eye and still not suffer from impaired vision. VERONICA LAKE

My acting range? Left eyebrow raised, right eyebrow raised. ROGER MOORE

I'm a whore. All actors are whores. We sell our bodies to the highest bidder. WILLIAM HOLDEN

Some people have youth, some have beauty. I have menace. EDWARD G. ROBINSON

I'm a meathead. I can't help it, man. You've got smart people and you've got dumb people. KEANU REEVES

I was not successful as a ball player, as it was a game of skill. CASEY STENGEL

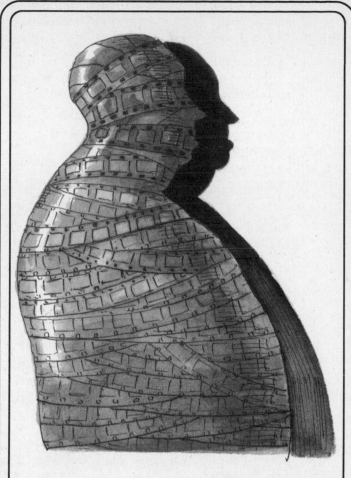

I've become a body of films, not a man. I am all those films. ALFRED HITCHCOCK

I fit the part of a disabled genius. At least I'm disabled—even though I'm not a genius like Einstein.   STEPHEN HAWKING

I am one of those unhappy persons who inspire bores to the highest flights of art.
EDITH SITWELL

I'm obviously a homosexual writer with hardly a woman in his books.
WILLIAM S. BURROUGHS

I'm old. I'm young. I'm intelligent. I'm stupid. My tide goes in and out.   WARREN BEATTY

I have a morbid sense of humor.
INGMAR BERGMAN

I think on some level I must be monumentally unsophisticated.   SALLY FIELD

I don't think I am any good. If I thought I was any good, I wouldn't be.   JOHN BETJEMAN

When I'm good I'm very good, but when I'm bad I'm better.   MAE WEST

I liked myself better when I wasn't me.
CAROL BURNETT

I'm nuts and I know it. But so long as I make 'em laugh, they ain't going to lock me up.

RED SKELTON

I am one of those fellows who have few adventures. I always get to the fire after it's out.

EDGAR RICE BURROUGHS

I'm no Shakespeare, no Hugo, no Balzac. Something a little higher than a louse. That's not overestimating myself, is it?

HENRY MILLER

I didn't go out of my way to get into this movie stuff. I think of myself as a writer.

SAM SHEPARD

I have been called a Rogue Elephant, a Cannibal Shark, and a Crocodile. I am none the worse. I remain a caged, and rather sardonic, Lion in a particularly contemptible and ill-run zoo.

PERCY WYNDHAM-LEWIS

I'm the Connie Francis of rock 'n' roll.

ELTON JOHN

I'm the Beatles of the opera.   BEVERLY SILLS

I'm in a class by myself, along with people like Rod Stewart.   ENGELBERT HUMPERDINCK

I think I've stretched a talent which is so thin it's almost transparent over a quite unbelievable term of years.   BING CROSBY

I am never quite sure if I am one of the cinema's elder statesmen or just the oldest whore on the beat.   JOSEPH L. MANKIEWICZ

I'm a fellow who works in the vineyard of compromise.   REP. DAN ROSTENKOWSKI

I am only a picture taster, the way others are wine or tea tasters.   BERNARD BERENSON

I'm not a fighter, I have bad reflexes. I was once run over by a car being pushed by two guys.   WOODY ALLEN

I knew twenty or thirty words of English from American talking pictures. It was too late for me to learn English without an accent. Now, after fifty years, I have a curious accent, which is a mixture of Arnold Schwartzenegger and Archbishop Tutu.   BILLY WILDER

I can't play a loser. I don't look like one.   ROCK HUDSON

I became one of the stately homos of England.   QUENTIN CRISP

There's something about me that makes a lot
of people want to throw up.   PAT BOONE

You think I'm an asshole now? You should've
seen me when I was drunk.
        JOHN COUGAR MELLENCAMP

I'm a sort of the boy next door. If that boy has
a good scriptwriter.   MICHAEL CAINE

I'm not crazy, but I think everyone else is.
            PETER O'TOOLE

I'm complicated, sentimental, lovable, honest,
loyal, decent, generous, likable, and lonely.
My personality is not split; it's shredded.
            JACK PAAR

I remain just one thing and one thing only—
and that is a clown. It places me on a far
higher plane than any politician.
        CHARLIE CHAPLIN

I am Mr. Mayer's little hunchback.
            JUDY GARLAND

I am the type of guy who'd sell you a rat's
asshole for a wedding ring.   TOM WAITS

I've made an ass of myself so many times I
often wonder if I am one.   NORMAN MAILER

I was a personality before I became a person—
I am simple, complex, generous, selfish, unat-
tractive, beautiful, lazy and driven.

BARBRA STREISAND

> I bear no grudges. My heart is as big as the
> sky and I have a mind that retains absolutely
> nothing.   BETTE MIDLER

I don't go in for this Method-acting stuff. It's
like playing all day long to me. So many of
these people take this shit so serious. First of
all, I'm not even that good of an actress. Second of all, I don't even want to be. I'm never
going to be a Meryl Streep. But then, she'll
never be a Dolly Parton either.

DOLLY PARTON

> I am an idealist without illusions.
>   JOHN F. KENNEDY

I'm clearly not a major legal genius.
JOHN F. KENNEDY, JR., after failing
the New York bar exam for
the second time

> Deep down, I'm pretty superficial.
>   AVA GARDNER

I'm an extinct volcano. NANCY ASTOR

I'm just a hoofer with a spare set of tails.

FRED ASTAIRE

I'm always amazed that people take what I say seriously. I don't even take what I *am* seriously.

DAVID BOWIE

I have all the shyness of the very vain.

V. S. NAIPAUL

I always thought I was Jeanne d'Arc and Bonaparte. How little one knows oneself.

CHARLES DE GAULLE

I know my limitations. I could never make it as a writer, and I could never make it as a fine artist. Thus the world of cartooning was waiting for me to come along. I have plenty of partial ability.

BERKE BREATHED

I'll never be a proper father or a great lover or an extraordinary boxer or a capable skier or an astronaut. Those are all the things I'm missing.

PAUL NEWMAN

The way I see things, the way I interpret things, is influenced by television. Visual conception, fast pace, quick cuts. I can't help it. I'm a product of the television age.

GEORGE LUCAS

I'm an alcoholic. I'm a drug addict. I'm a homosexual. I'm a genius.   TRUMAN CAPOTE

I'm outside of the system.   WAYLON JENNINGS

I'm a tuning fork, tense and twanging all the
time.   EDNA O'BRIEN

I am married to Beatrice Salkeld, a painter. We
have no children, except me.
                               BRENDAN BEHAN

My Own Worst Enemy

Looking back, my life seems like one long obstacle race, with me as its chief obstacle.

JACK PAAR

I'm so gullible. I'm so damn gullible. And I am so *sick* of me being gullible.   LANA TURNER

When I make a mistake, it's a beaut.

FIORELLO LAGUARDIA

I'm not into character assassination, except my own.   CARRIE FISHER

In life . . . I feel like I fall short in just about everything. In music I can just about do what I need to do. I feel pretty calm most of the time, but then if I review my situation at all, it always seems like I'm up there walking the plank. I'm probably a driven person. I always feel like somebody's cracking the whip. Somebody or something.   BOB DYLAN

My instincts stink . . . Hollywood, the marriages, the divorces, a limo and a yacht. I actually had a yacht, and on the first trip we were thirteen feet out and my father and brother started vomiting. SYLVESTER STALLONE

I have problems flown in fresh daily wherever
I am.   RICHARD LEWIS

Sometimes I'm so sweet even I can't stand
it.   JULIE ANDREWS

My vigor, vitality and cheek repel me. I am the
kind of woman I would run away from.
                                    NANCY ASTOR

With me, it's just a genetic dissatisfaction with
everything.   WOODY ALLEN

I can't stand myself. I don't like anything I've
done.   TONY RANDALL

I don't remember anyone who could stand
being in my company for more than five hours
without running into the street.
                                    HARLAN ELLISON

I bring to my life a certain amount of
mess.   FRANCIS COPPOLA

As a confirmed melancholic, I can testify that
the best and maybe only antidote for melan-
cholia is *action*. However, like most melan-
cholics, I suffer also from sloth.
                                    EDWARD ABBEY

I have the true feeling of myself only when I am unbearably unhappy. FRANZ KAFKA

> My main problem during a fight was that I couldn't truly get angry, even when it seemed my life was at stake. It was all play-acting with me. It mattered and it didn't.
> CHARLES BUKOWSKI

I am a spy in the house of me. I report back from the front lines of the battle that is me. I am somewhat nonplussed by the event that is my life. CARRIE FISHER

Madonna
Our Lady of Perpetual Confession

PART II

I have to schedule everything, and that drives everyone I'm with insane. *Everyone.* They go, "Can't you just wake up in the morning and not plan your day? Can't you just be spontaneous?" And I just can't.

My life is splayed out for the world to see.

They [the technicians on the set] don't see me as an actress, they see me as an icon, and it makes me extremely exhausted.

I *live* for meetings with suits. I love them because I know they had a really boring week and I walk in there with my orange velvet leggings and drop popcorn in my cleavage and then fish it out and eat it. I like that. I know I'm entertaining them and I know that they know.

My whole life is in a constant state of disarray, and the one thing that doesn't change is the workout.... If you're feeling depressed about something, you get on the Lifecycle and you forget it.

MADONNA

Everyone that is employed by me signs a privacy contract, from my maid to a backup singer. It's a way of protecting myself before I get to know people and know that I can trust them.

I'm hardest on myself.

Even when I feel
like shit, they still love me.

I can throw
a fit, I'm a master at it.

I l-o-o-ove to read.

I think
I've met everybody.

I've never
had a Quaalude.

I'm very maternal with people. Like with the dancers in the movie [*Truth or Dare*]: I mother them all during the movie and I still do. Still! I'm still very close to them and completely embroiled in their lives and trying to help them. In addition to that, I have my own, very large family, who are all emotional cripples in one way or another. So I'm the matriarch of all these little families. I can't keep my hand out of the fire. I just keep getting pulled into everyone's lives and try to help them out of their messes. Meanwhile, I'm neglecting all of my own. So ... my life remains completely insane. Don't let this calm facade fool you.

I always make the Worst-Dressed List. It is kind of nice having something you can count on.

I dreamt once that I had composed a piece of music all notes of which were to be cooked and then eaten. On the way to the concert hall to perform this piece, I stopped to rehearse and cooked the notes. Then around came a bunch of dogs and cats and ate them all up!

JOHN CAGE

When I was an utter flop, I kept having the same dream—that all my teeth were falling out.

ENGELBERT HUMPERDINCK

The worst nightmare I ever had about Vietnam was that I had to go back. It was a couple of years ago. I woke up in a sweat, in total terror.

OLIVER STONE

Sometimes in my dreams there are women. When such dreams happen, immediately I remember: "I am a monk."

DALAI LAMA

Last night I dreamed of a small consolation enjoyed only by the blind: Nobody knows the trouble I've *not* seen! JAMES THURBER

In my waking hours in London I saw myself as Joel McCrea in *Foreign Correspondent*, wearing a double-breasted trench coat and hiding in windmills. I finally realized I was Perelman from Providence, Rhode Island.

S. J. PERELMAN

I'd like to put on buckskins and a ponytail and go underwater with a reed, hiding from the Indians. I'd love to be pushing off a birchbark canoe in a forest. To me, that's sexy!

KEVIN COSTNER

Valentino silently acted out the fantasies of women all over the world. Valentino and his world were a dream. A whole generation of females wanted to ride off to a sandy paradise with him. At thirteen I had been such a female. BETTE DAVIS

Barbara Stanwyck is my favorite. My God, I could just sit and dream of being married to her, having a little cottage out in the hills, vines around the door. I'd come home from the office tired and weary, and I'd be met by Barbara, walking through the door holding an apple pie she had cooked herself. And wearing no drawers. HERMAN MANKIEWICZ

I'd like to have made one of those big, splashy Technicolor musicals with Rita Hayworth.

CARY GRANT

> I used to dream of being normal. For me, if Sammy Davis or Kirk Douglas walked into the house, that was normal. So the outside world seemed exotic to me. And when I first moved out of our home in Benedict Canyon, I moved to a little house in the San Fernando Valley. That was my dream—a home in suburbia.
>
> JAMIE LEE CURTIS

In my room as a kid, I used to create an atmosphere of the ring. I'd play a fighter and get knocked to the floor and come back to win.

DUSTIN HOFFMAN

Epiphanies

All the muddy waters of my life cleared up when I gave myself to Christ. MICKEY ROONEY

When I found the trumpet, I found the best part of me.   DIZZY GILLESPIE

Looking up at my horrible, ugly bulk on a huge screen was the turning point in my life.
LYNN REDGRAVE

It was revealed to me many years ago with conclusive certainty that I was a fool and that I had always been a fool. Since then I have been as happy as any man has a right to be.   ALASTAIR SIM

In my youth I stressed freedom, and in my old age I stress order. I have made the great discovery that liberty is a product of order.
WILL DURANT

I stopped believing in Santa Claus when I was six. Mother took me to see him in a department store and he asked me for my autograph.

SHIRLEY TEMPLE

I had no idea what it would be like to have a baby. It was a complete shock to me—that I would have such deep feelings, and that she would be so much fun.   BETTE MIDLER

When I first read about my mother and Sinatra in Kitty Kelley's book, I thought, Well, God, I spent the whole evening with him and he never came on to me. . . . And then I thought, Maybe he did come on to me and I just didn't recognize it. Maybe there was something to all those singing lessons after all.   PATTI DAVIS

I believe that the power to make money is a gift from God.   JOHN D. ROCKEFELLER

I've been forty years discovering that the queen of all colors is black.
PIERRE AUGUSTE RENOIR

I gave up being serious about making pictures around the time I made a film with Greer Garson and she took a hundred and twenty-five takes to say no.   ROBERT MITCHUM

When I drove through the studio gate and the thrill was gone, I knew it was time to quit.
JAMES CAGNEY

I knew I needed help when drugs became more important in my life than my music.

DAVID CROSBY

I've come to the realization that I have absolutely no idea what I'm doing half the time.

DAVID BOWIE

I'm originally from Iowa. It took a long time for me to realize we were free to go.

JAKE JOHANNSEN

G. GORDON LIDDY
Fear and Suffering

From playmates who were German, I learned some of the language. One day our German maid Teresa was excited. *He* was going to be on the radio. Just wait till I hear him speak! Eagerly, I joined her at the Emerson. First the music, the now familiar strains of a song that started, *"Die Fahne hoch . . ."*—"Raise the banner . . ." It was a rousing, powerful anthem, the Horst Wessel song.

We could tell when *he* was about to speak. The crowd could hardly contain itself. They hailed him in huge, swelling ovations that carried me along. *"Sieg!"* someone would shout, and what seemed like all the people in the world would answer with a roar, *"Heil!"* For *he* was their leader, *Der Führer*, Adolf Hitler.

Hitler's voice started out calmly, in low, dispassionate tones, but as he spoke of what his people would accomplish, his voice rose in pitch and tempo. Once united, the German people could do anything, surmount any obstacle, rout any enemy, achieve fulfillment. He would lead them; there would be one people, one nation, one leader. Here was the very antithesis of fear—sheer animal confidence and power of will. He sent an electric current through my body, and as the massive audience thundered its absolute support and determination, the hair on the back of my neck rose and I realized suddenly that I had stopped breathing.

When I spoke of this man to my father, he became angry. Adolf Hitler, he said, was an evil man who would once again set loose upon the world all the destruction of war. It was just a matter of time. I was to stop listening to him.

The lure of forbidden fruit was too strong; I continued to listen, though less frequently. Teresa had said that Adolf Hitler had raised her country from the dead, freed it from its enemies, made it the strongest nation in the world and delivered it from fear. *Delivered it from fear!*

For the first time in my life I felt hope. Life need *not* be a constant secret agony of fear and shame. If an entire nation could be changed, lifted out of weakness to extraordinary strength, certainly so could one person.

At Mass on Sunday I'd been taught that human beings are created "in the image and likeness of God." But God did not fear; he was all-powerful and could do anything just by thinking about it. Obviously, in my case, an error had been made. But God did not make mistakes. Besides, there was the example of all my relatives. I was of the same blood. The answer was obvious; the error was mine, the *fault* was mine. Since the error was mine, if I were to change, the changing would have to be mine. Alone. I could not *be* changed, there was no one to do it for me.

I knew what I had to do, and I dreaded it. To change myself from a puny, fearful boy to a strong, fearless man, I would have to face my fears, one by one, and overcome them. From listening to the priests at Sunday Mass, I knew that would take willpower. Even Adolf Hitler agreed. He and his people would triumph through the power of their superior will. But I knew from the priests the price would be terrible. God gave us a free will, but to strengthen that will to meet the temptations of life required denial, "mortification," suffering.

Suffering. That was the key. Whatever the consequences of what I was to do, I must accept and endure them—*out-last* suffering to achieve my goals. Wasn't that the message of my mother's stories? Of President Roosevelt? My fears were so many and so gripping that overcoming them, one by one, would build incredible willpower! The world opened up to me. *I could become anything I wanted to be!* The thought took my breath away.

Teresa had told me of the Germans' suffering before their rebirth; my mother had told me how the strength and bravery of the American Indian warriors was born of the suffering of torture. In the Book of Knowledge I had read of the Spartan boy who refused to cry out while a fox concealed beneath his clothing ate the boy's insides—and thus the boy had died a true Spartan. Hadn't Glenn Cunningham suffered as he stretched the scar tissue of his burned legs to run faster? Hadn't my grandfather suffered to return to play football with only one eye? *Had not Jesus suffered the agony of hanging nailed to a cross for three hours before He could triumph over death?*

To face each of my fears and overcome them would require years of psychic and physical pain. But it had to be done. I had seen the fruits of fearlessness and the power of the will. I could no longer live without them. It was 1936, and I was almost six years old.

Obsessions and Compulsions

When the light goes on in the refrigerator, I do twenty minutes.
JERRY LEWIS

My whole life revolves around dessert.
MARVIN HAMLISCH

I think of ties morning, noon and night. If I have insomnia, I count ties instead of sheep.
COUNTESS MARA

I just love, I *love*, I love movies.   LAURA DERN

I always had one ear offstage, listening for the call from the bookie.   WALTER MATTHAU

I propose to anybody. I say it to a hatcheck girl. I say it to anybody ... sort of as a form of introduction.   TOMMY MANVILLE

I'm the worst person to be stuck with in a traffic jam. I start pounding the wheel, honking the horn, looking for a way out. If I can't find a moving lane, I start climbing the walls, which isn't easy in an automobile.

LARRY KING

I used to eat my eyebrows. Until I was eleven or twelve I sucked my thumb and pulled at my eyebrows with my fingers. Sometimes I would put honey or something sweet on them, then pluck them and play with them in my mouth.

NASTASSIA KINSKI

I used to pick my navel, and I used to pick it until it bled.

MARIETTE HARTLEY

At 6:00 A.M. I always feel I should be up and doing something productive.

ARNOLD SCHWARZENEGGER

Even if I set out to make a film about filet of sole, it would be about me.

FEDERICO FELLINI

Creation is a drug I can't do without.

CECIL B. DE MILLE

I am not interested in relationships of color or anything else—I am interested only in expressing the basic human emotions—tragedy, ecstasy, doom.

MARK ROTHKO

I'm full of fears and I do my best to avoid difficulties and any kind of complications. I like everything around me to be clear as crystal and completely calm. I don't want clouds overhead. I get a feeling of inner peace from a well-organized desk. When I take a bath, I put everything neatly back in place. You wouldn't even know I'd been in the bathroom. My passion for orderliness goes hand in hand with a strong revulsion toward complications.

ALFRED HITCHCOCK

I never forget what I eat! I still remember what Marlon [Brando] served me on our first date: cold cauliflower salad and cheap bourbon.

SHELLEY WINTERS

People invite me to dinner not because I cook, but because I like to clean up. I get immediate gratification from Windex. Yes, I do windows.

CAROL BURNETT

I watch eighty to ninety hours of TV if I can. I even enjoy the Weather Channel. I keep the television on at night. It's always on. I watch all the trash. I watch everything.

HARRY NILSSON

Sheets are very important to me! The feel of good sheets!

CARLY SIMON

I spend a lot of time thinking what it would be like to be other people.   ERIC BOGOSIAN

I've discovered I've got this preoccupation with ordinary people pursued by large forces.   STEVEN SPIELBERG

I always had a repulsive sort of need to be something more than human.   DAVID BOWIE

I don't need to be Tom Cruise. I just need to work forever.   JODIE FOSTER

I need to be in the country.   JOHNNY CASH

Dirty Little Secrets

I don't think the intelligence reports are all that hot. Some days I get more out of the *New York Times*.
JOHN F. KENNEDY

When the late President Kennedy was revealed as a speed reader, it took me three hours to read the article about it.
OSCAR LEVANT

I really liked Lassie, but that horse Flicka was a nasty animal with a terrible disposition. All the Flickas—all six of them—were awful.
RODDY MCDOWALL

Sometimes at the end of the day when I'm smiling and shaking hands, I want to kick them.
RICHARD NIXON

I used to be a lawyer, but now I am a reformed character.
WOODROW WILSON

I used to be Snow White, but I drifted.

MAE WEST

If the FBI went back far enough, I was always suspect: I never liked football.

DANIEL BERRIGAN

When I got out of high school they retired my jersey, but it was for hygiene and sanitary reasons.

GEORGE CARLIN

I don't like baths. I don't enjoy them in the slightest and, if I could, I'd prefer to go around dirty.

J. B. PRIESTLEY

A man of my standing and upbringing certainly isn't going to wash his own underwear, so I do a second time around on the dirties. Then I go to KMart and buy a six-month supply of undershorts.

LEWIS GRIZZARD

I have never sat down in my tux pants, never in my career.

JERRY LEWIS

When it came to writing about wine, I did what almost everybody else does—faked it.

ART BUCHWALD

I like to pretend that my art has nothing to do with me.

ROY LICHTENSTEIN

Do you remember when everyone began ana-
lyzing Beatle songs? I don't think I understood
what some of them were supposed to be
about.   RINGO STARR

I don't think I've used a hanger in my entire
life. I have always enjoyed living in my own
debris.   STEVEN SPIELBERG

When I wake up in the morning, I think of me
first and then my wife and then my children.
I'd like to meet the guy that can honestly
admit he does differently.   JERRY LEWIS

I must confess that at the very beginning when the Special Theory of Relativity began to germinate in me, I was visited by all sorts of nervous conflicts. When young I used to go away for weeks in a state of confusion, as one who at that time had yet to overcome the state of stupefaction in his first encounter with such questions.   ALBERT EINSTEIN

Everybody thinks I'm self-assured. I'm so insecure that when I enter a room I'll lay back until I see a friendly face. I may not want them fifteen minutes later, but right then I need them.   LEONA HELMSLEY

I had nothing to offer anybody except my own confusion.   JACK KEROUAC

Sometimes I worry about being a success in a mediocre world.   LILY TOMLIN

I have this terrible fear that I'm going to be forced to take a general knowledge test in public. DICK CAVETT

I'm scared to death of audiences.

JOHNNY MATHIS

Sometimes I wake up about 4:00 A.M. and I'm scared for a minute, because I wonder where the hell I am.   WARREN BEATTY

Aggressive feminists scare me.   OMAR SHARIF

I write in terror. I have to talk myself into bravery with every sentence, sometimes every syllable. I have a raven perched on my right shoulder at all times that says, "That's not good, that's ugly."   CYNTHIA OZICK

I don't have big anxieties. I wish I did. I'd be much more interesting.   ROY LICHTENSTEIN

I have a dread of being considered bland.

GEORGE SEGAL

I'm afraid of losing my obscurity. Genuineness only thrives in the dark.   ALDOUS HUXLEY

I am but too conscious of the fact that we are born in an age when only the dull are treated seriously, and I live in terror of not being misunderstood.   OSCAR WILDE

I think in twenty years I'll be looked at like Bob Hope. Doing these president jokes and golf jokes. It scares me.   EDDIE MURPHY

I don't mind being regarded as perverted and unnatural, but I would *die* if people thought I was a Democrat.   FLORENCE KING

Every time I tell somebody how much it frightens me to ride in an airplane and how afraid I am it will fall out of the sky and I will die, they say, "Don't panic." I panic dialing for reservations.   LEWIS GRIZZARD

I'm scared to death of being stone cold sober.   JERRY LEE LEWIS

I'm scared of electricity. Every time I plug something in, I think I'm going to die. I'm scared to turn the heat on ... because I'm afraid the house will blow up.   JOHN WATERS

I can't stand nobody touching my toes. I have a real phobia about it. Like at night when I sleep, I have to have my toes sticking out from the sheet. I can't have them covered. That drives me berserk.   ROSEANNE BARR

I have three phobias which, could I mute them, would make my life as slick as a sonnet, but as dull as ditch water: I hate to go to bed, I hate to get up, and I hate to be alone.

TALLULAH BANKHEAD

I have a horror of sunsets. They are so romantic, so operatic.

MARCEL PROUST

My problem is that I carry around such a load of nonspecific guilt that every time the metal detector beeps, I always have a wild fear that this trip I absentmindedly packed a Luger.

DAN GREENBURG

I don't want to go to jail because I'm afraid of lesbians.

ZSA ZSA GABOR

I do not fear death, I only fear sleep. I want to know what is happening to me.

CHARLES DE GAULLE

I get extremely nervous in sales situations. I will do absolutely anything to please the salesperson. Usually, in stores, I can flee on foot before a salesperson gets to me, but if I don't get away, I'm a dead man. Like, if I'm walking through Sears, and I happen to pause for just a moment in the major appliances section, and one of those Sears appliance salespersons in polyester sport jackets comes sidling up and says, "Can I help you?" I instantly go into a state of extreme anxiety and say: "Yes, I'll take one of these, please," pointing to whatever major appliance I happen to be standing in front of, even though we probably already have one.   DAVE BARRY

I fear Allah, thunderstorms and bad airplane rides.   MUHAMMAD ALI

I do not fear computers. I fear the lack of them.   ISAAC ASIMOV

I'm an incredibly selfish and insecure person. I fear the future.   JULIE CHRISTIE

Am I afraid of high notes? Of course I am afraid! What sane man is not?
                    LUCIANO PAVAROTTI

JOHN UPDIKE
Getting the Words Out

The Jerusalem *Post* of November 10, 1978, having attacked my rumpled attire after I'd lost my luggage, went on to expose my stutter: "Updike has the slight slurp of a speech impediment, the sort of thing once affected by cavalry subalterns." I liked to imagine, all evidence to the contrary, that it, like my deplorable skin, was unnoticeable—that only I was conscious of it. Conscious, that is, of a kind of windowpane suddenly inserted in front of my face while I was talking, or of an obdurate barrier thrust into my throat. My first memory of the sensation is associated with our Shillington neighbor Eddie Pritchard, a somewhat larger boy than I whom I was trying, on the sidewalk in front of our houses, to reason into submission. I think he was calling me "Ostrich," a nickname I did not think I deserved, and a fear of being misunderstood or mistaken for somebody else has accompanied the impediment ever since. There seems so much about me to explain—all of it subsumable under the heading of "I am not an ostrich"—that when freshly encountering, say, a bored and hurried electrician over the telephone, my voice tends to seize up. If the electrician has already been to the house, the seizing up is less dramatic, and if I encounter not his voice but that of his maternal-sounding secretary, I become quite vocal—indeed, something of a minor virtuoso of the spoken language. For there is no doubt that I have lots of words inside me; but at moments, like rush-hour traffic at the mouth of a tunnel, they jam.

It happens when I feel myself in a false position. My worst recent public collapse, that I can bear to remember, came at a May meeting of the august American Academy and Institute of Arts and Letters, when I tried to read a number of award citations—hedgy and bloated, as citations tend to be—that I had not written. I could scarcely push and batter my way through the politic words, and a woman in the audience loudly laughed, as if I were doing an "act." Similarly, many years before, one spring evening, on the stage of the Shillington High School auditorium, I (I, who played the father in our class plays, who was on the debating team, who gave droll "chalk talks" with aplomb even in other county high schools) could barely get out a few formal words in my capacity as class president. I did not, at heart, feel I deserved to be class president (whereas I did somehow deserve to give the chalk talks), and in protest at my false position my vocal apparatus betrayed me. In most people there is a settled place they speak from; in me it remains unsettled, unfinished, provisional. Viewing myself on taped television, I see the repulsive symptoms of an approaching stammer take possession of my face—an electronically rapid flutter of the eyelashes, a distortion of the mouth as of a leather purse being cinched, a terrified hardening of the upper lip, a fatal tensing and lifting of the voice. And through it all a detestable coyness and craven willingness to please, to assure my talk-show host and his millions of viewers that I am not, appearances to the contrary, an ostrich.

As with my psoriasis, the affliction is perhaps not entirely unfortunate. It makes me think twice about going on stage and appearing in classrooms and at conferences—all that socially approved yet spiritually corrupting public talking that writers of even modest note are asked to do. Being obliging by nature and anxious for social approval, I would never say no if I weren't afraid of stuttering. Also, as I judge from my own reactions, people who talk too easily and comfortably, with too much happy rolling of the vowels and satisfied curling of the lips around the grammatical rhythms, rouse distrust in some atavistic, pre-speech part of ourselves; we turn off. Whereas those who stutter win, in the painful pauses of their demonstration that speech isn't entirely natural, a respectful attention, a tender alertness. Words are, we are reassured, precious.

Wretched Excess

I hate possessions but I have to have houses because I have to have books. I buy houses to put the books in. I once had a house on the Hudson, a Greek temple built in 1820. I finally sold it and got rid of everything. I found that I owned forty-two sofas. Just think of that. I do not have sofas now.   GORE VIDAL

The post is hopeless and I have given up sending things by post. I have things delivered in my Rolls.   BARBARA CARTLAND

I tend to buy cars for the fun of it. I drive them around for three weeks and then I get bored, dump them in the garage and let the batteries go completely flat.   EDDIE MURPHY

I have a lust for diamonds, almost like a disease.   ELIZABETH TAYLOR

I like Pratesi, Shaxteds and Grand Maison de Blanc. I buy one really nice set a year, because if I told my husband how much they cost, he'd kill me! I've been buying them for the last twenty years, so I have a beautiful collection. I love hand-embroidered sheets, but not all cotton, because I don't like it when they're wrinkled—a nice blend is fine. And I like them freshly laundered.　　CRISTINA FERRARE

There was a time when I heard eleven operas in a fortnight . . . which left me bankrupt and half-idiotic for a month.　　　J. B. PRIESTLEY

I hate to advocate drugs, alcohol, violence, or insanity to anyone, but they've always worked for me.　　　HUNTER S. THOMPSON

I've had eighteen straight whiskies. I think that's the record.　　　DYLAN THOMAS

My weakness is wearing too much leopard print.　　　JACKIE COLLINS

I have enough fruitcakes in my freezer to enlarge my patio.　　　ERMA BOMBECK

I gotta tell ya, with our $2.4 billion in profits last year, they gave me a great big bonus. Really, it's almost obscene.　　　LEE IACOCCA

I've married a few people I shouldn't have, but haven't we all?　　　MAMIE VAN DOREN

Wretched Excess—129

Odd Jobs

I was a telephone salesman pitching light bulbs. It was 1976, and I was just looking for some grocery money. I hated the job, it was horrible. It was all lying, outrageous prices and phony names. I called myself Dave Wilson— you had to come up with a name so people would *think* they knew you. I'd call and say, "Hey, Bill, remember I talked to you eighteen months ago? It's Dave Wilson." And the other person doesn't want to insult me, so they'd say, "Yeah, I think I remember." I only had the job a couple of weeks and knew it was time to leave as soon as I could afford a loaf of bread.   JERRY SEINFELD

I was a lousy accountant. I always figured that if you came within eight bucks of what you needed you were doing okay. I made up the difference out of my own pocket.

BOB NEWHART

When I was [at the Associated Press] all I did was sit in a small, windowless office and rewrite stories out of the *Philadelphia Bulletin.* . . . I almost never went outside the actual building except to put money in the parking meter. If I had seen a nuclear mushroom cloud rising over downtown Philadelphia, my reaction, as a newsman, would have been: "Huh! I hope the Bulletin comes out soon, so I can report this!"   DAVE BARRY

I made appearances at cocktail parties in Florida for $500 a pop, pretending to be an old friend of the host.   MICKEY ROONEY

I was in the CIA.   WILLIAM F. BUCKLEY, JR.

If Hollywood didn't work out, I was all prepared to be the best secretary in the world.
          BETTE DAVIS

I gave my best performances, perhaps, during the war—trying to be an officer and a gentleman.   ALEC GUINNESS

In Hawaii I was the chief chunker in a pineapple canning factory. I used to come home smelling like a compote.   BETTE MIDLER

I was fired from my job at a Howard Johnson's when somebody asked me the ice cream flavor of the week and I said, "Chicken."
          MIKE NICHOLS

MADONNA
Our Lady of Perpetual Confession

PART III

All of my sexual experiences when I was young were with girls. I mean, we didn't have those sleep-over parties for nothing. I think that's really normal: same-sex experimentation. You get really curious, and there's your girlfriend, and she's spending the night with you, and it happens.

Losing my
virginity was a career move.

I never like to have a crush on somebody everybody else has a crush on.

I've never
owned a vibrator.

Effeminate men intrigue me more than anything in the world. I see them as my alter egos. I feel very drawn to them. I think

My sexual image is looming out there in front of me. Everyone probably thinks that I'm a raving nymphomaniac, that I have an insatiable sexual appetite, when the truth is I'd rather read a book.   MADONNA

like a guy, but I'm feminine. So I relate to feminine men.

I'm aroused by the idea of a woman making love to me while either a man or another woman watches. Is that kinky?

The fact is, [Sandra Bernhard] is a great friend of mine. Whether I'm gay or not is irrelevant. Whether I slept with her or not is irrelevant. I'm perfectly willing to have people think that I did. You know, I do not want to protest too much. I don't care. If it makes people feel better to think that I slept with her, then they can think it. And if it makes them feel safer to think that I didn't, then that's fine too.

You know, I'd almost rather they thought that I did. Just so they could know that here was this girl that everyone was buying records of, and she was eating someone's pussy. So there.

I think I've only been in love with men, because ultimately the approval I seek is my father's.

Power is a great aphrodisiac and I'm a very powerful person.

Trough Experiences

On a fine December day in 1924, as I walked down Hollywood Boulevard toward nowhere in particular, I was down to that essential starting place for actors. I was broke.

GARY COOPER

There were times when my pants were so thin, I could sit on a dime and know if it was heads or tails. SPENCER TRACY

Once, during Prohibition, I was forced to live on nothing but food and water. W. C. FIELDS

Starting with a very modest advance from my publisher, I rose to near-millionaire status, then plummeted to my current state of affairs, which recently saw me borrow a few dollars from my father to fix the muffler on my car—all in eight years. PHILIP CAPUTO

I couldn't get any jobs, and when that happens, you get so humble it's disgusting. I didn't feel like a man anymore—I felt really creepy. I was bumping into walls and saying, "Excuse me." JOE PESCI

There were a few hustlers who depended upon finding suckers for survival. And there were some who were too wise to hustle, who only wanted to have enough money to be able to afford to be a sucker. DUKE ELLINGTON

I would lose ten or fifteen pounds in a week, eating nothing but cucumbers and working all day. My hands would shake all the time, and sometimes I'd pass out. But then I would go on these enormous binges. I lived alone and was very lonely. I made myself spaghetti dinners and chocolate cake and ate the whole thing, then tried to throw up because I was in such pain. But I couldn't. My body would be so swollen the next day that it would hurt to touch, and my eyes would be little slits. SALLY FIELD

You want to hear about insanity? I was found running naked through the jungles in Mexico. At the Mexico City airport I decided I was in the middle of a movie and walked out on the wing on takeoff. My body . . . my liver . . . okay, my brain . . . went. DENNIS HOPPER

Once I started using drugs, I just didn't *stop*. My first marriage was ruined by that. I almost lost my son for being a negligent mother. My mother and I weren't speaking. I had to sign over my estate to her because I wasn't capable of handling my own affairs.   NATALIE COLE

There have been times when I've prayed for a bus to hit me so I'd have an excuse not to perform.   LINDA RONSTADT

After years of advising other people on their personal problems, I was stunned by my own divorce. I only wish I had someone to write to for help.   ANN LANDERS

It is true that when I was fourteen years old I became pregnant. The baby was born prematurely and died shortly after birth. The experience was the most emotional, confusing and traumatic of my young life.   OPRAH WINFREY

It really shook me up when Trigger passed on. It was like losing one of the family.
                    ROY ROGERS

Early in my career I was in my dressing room making up. Suddenly I turned around and there was this totally naked woman. "What's the matter, dahling?" Tallulah Bankhead said. "Haven't you ever seen a blonde before?"
                DONALD SUTHERLAND

TAKI
Busted

The flight was perfect. I had a sound sleep and, upon arrival, was the first one out of the plane and through passport control, with no luggage except a small carry-on. The rest of my clothes were in my London flat. Passing through customs I was asked if I had anything to declare. I said I had nothing. The officer looked through my small bag and waved me on. Then, as I was leaving, I heard a voice say, "You're going to lose that envelope."

"Oh, thank you," I replied, being Taki, "if only you knew what was in it."

The man crooked his finger. "Come back here," he said.

And that was it.

The first thought that crossed my mind as I entered the cell was that life would never again be the same. The word *never* has a permanence I've always found hard to digest. On this occasion, however, I remember distinctly that I had absolutely no doubt that some terrible dark shadow had caught up with me for good. Yet, being under arrest is no big deal. I had once spent time in a Palestinian guerrilla jail somewhere in Jordan, and I had been held for two days by the Greek military police. Both arrests, however, were experiences that made me proud. They involved no shame or dishonor, certainly no feeling of humiliation. This, of course, was different. Not being someone who feels that possessing wealth or enjoying privilege is automatically wrong or guiltworthy, I had always refused to regard my hectic pursuit of adventure as necessarily venal. But now I had become one among many whose money and privileges had led them from self-indulgence to self-destructiveness to criminal misconduct.

The cell was located somewhere in the bowels of Heathrow Airport. As I waited for a body search, another thought flashed over me: my morbid fascination with danger was over. After a complete search, the officers read me my rights and the grilling began in earnest. It went on for ten hours. While it was still continuing, late in the afternoon, two agents drove into London and took apart my flat. They found nothing, and upon their return the atmosphere relaxed, the questioning became softer, less hostile. In fact, I was even offered a cup of tea. (I later found out that one of the officers who had searched my flat was a regular reader of my column.)

The grilling is just like the movies. One officer acts like Mr. Nice and the other threatens. Both my interrogators wanted to know who else I had taken cocaine with. That, I flatly refused to tell them. I did, however, tell them everything else: how many times I had bought it, if I had ever taken it across national boundaries, the amount I usually bought. I even gave them the name of the club where I had bought the stuff, but used a false name for the bar-man—in truth, I didn't know his real one. They repeated their early question a number of times: Who else had I taken cocaine with? There was no way I could or would answer. People who took coke were committing a victimless crime, and those who had taken it with me had done so in confidence. So, eventually, when the officers made their final offer, "Give us a couple of names and then you can go to the bathroom," I blurted out, for a joke, "Prince Charles and Prince Andrew." For a second they looked incredulous, and then they began to laugh. Soon after that we packed it up and headed for a police station, and a real prison cell.

Once there I was booked, fingerprinted and locked up for the night in a windowless cell. Needless to say, one does not sleep in prison on the first night. One paces up and down, and at times sideways, one counts the squares that make up the soundproof walls, plays games in which one wakes up suddenly and finds out it's been a bad dream.

Time, however, goes slowly. In fact, one feels like a passenger on an empty platform waiting for an urgent train that refuses to come. Every once in a while, someone clicks open the judas spyhole and checks that the inmate isn't attempting suicide.

As everything had been taken away from me I could tell time only by the activity I could hear outside. Finally, the door was banged open and someone told me to follow an officer. I did. We drove in a Black Maria for about half an hour and then, once again, I was put into a tiny cell and instructed to wait. About three hours later, an officer stopped by and asked me if I had a lawyer. I said no, and was assigned one by the court. Eventually he came in and I told him everything. I also asked him to make sure that no newspapers got hold of the story. He seemed like a nice man who knew his way around, and my spirits rose. But when I was ushered into a courtroom above the cells my heart sank. The whole press gallery was full; I could see some familiar faces among them.

I pleaded guilty to the charge of importing twenty grams of cocaine and then the officer who had busted me, a Mr. Richardson, took over. Richardson was the Mr. Bad Guy of the previous day. But he must have had either the most pleasant of dreams that night or a terrific bowel movement that morning, or both, because he turned out, now, to be all sweetness and light. He said he was convinced I was carrying the stuff for my personal use, that I had been cooperative and truthful, and for good measure he told the court how I had pretty much given myself away by volunteering the contents in the envelope even before any question of a search arose.

From the corner of my eye I noticed a couple of hacks sniggering. Then my lawyer got up and in two seconds flat I knew my next destination was definitely going to be indoors. Although I had instructed him not to mention that I was a writer, the presence of a small company of Fleet Street hacks made my request redundant. So he banged on about what an important journalist I was, how the pressure of my work had driven me to cocaine, and then, for good measure, he threw in the fact that I was almost as rich as the Queen herself. And, he went on to add, "In the group he runs around with, cocaine is considered a lesser evil than a good glass of red wine."

After that remark, of course, louder sniggering came from the press section. But the magistrate, who looked like a kind old boy, and the two ladies who made up the troika deciding my fate, neither approved nor were amused. Before they had a chance to say anything, I raised my hand and asked to be recognized. I was given a minute to confer with my lawyer. "He now tells me that cocaine is not as widely used as wine in his circle" was the way my counsellor put it when we resumed. More sniggering and a warning from the bench followed that pearl of wisdom. Finally, the three magistrates retired and I sat waiting while every pair of eyes in the room took in my unkempt appearance, which became more unkempt by the minute as I began to sweat profusely.

When they returned the old boy said, "The importing of cocaine into Britain is a serious offense. Although the defendant is of previous good character, and the court is convinced the cocaine was meant for his personal use, I nevertheless sentence you to four months in prison."

I was then taken back into the cells while my attorney appealed, and I posted bail pending that appeal. By mid-afternoon I was free, and I drove into London, five pounds thinner and five thousand pounds poorer. The English summer was just beginning, but to me it felt like the last days of autumn— gloomy, depressing and fraught with a sense of foreboding.

Shame on me

Near our vineyard there was a pear tree laden with fruit that was not attractive in either flavor or form. One night, when I [at the age of sixteen] had played until dark on the sandlot with some other juvenile delinquents, we went to shake that tree and carry off its fruit. From it we carried off huge loads, not to feast on, but to throw to the pigs, although we did eat a few ourselves. We did it just because it was forbidden. — SAINT AUGUSTINE

When I was a kid, there was a time when I shot anything that couldn't tell on me. I must have killed a thousand birds, no reason except the killing. I think back on that now, and I don't know how I could have done that, or why. I just know that something was in me then that went away. — PETE DEXTER

I once spray-painted the back of the replica of Rodin's *The Thinker* in front of the Detroit Art Museum with these provocative words:

"WHAT'S THIS PIG THINKING ABOUT? THE TIME FOR REVOLUTION IS NOW!" ANDREI CODRESCU

For some reason, mothers with nursing babies liked to sit down front near the piano. Maybe they thought that music was a nice, soothing accompaniment to breast feeding. Anyway, I used to have fun with them. In the middle of a quiet scene I'd suddenly whack the hell out of a chord, just to watch the nipples snap out of the babies' mouths. HARPO MARX

When it got to the point where I couldn't pay the rent, I got a little hysterical and robbed. . . . I had four kids. . . . What was I going to do? I should have been put away for what I did.
DANNY AIELLO

I've spread my legs in the backseat in a creative sense quite a few times. STEPHEN KING

I nearly fainted with rage and frustration. Who the hell had arranged the rooms! Wasn't I as good as Bogie! I went to the manager. No reaction. Then I asked who else in the company was housed there. I found that the accountant and auditor, who had been there for some time, had a lovely room next to the Bogarts. Without a wasted step, without a thought of them or their rights of possession, and certainly with not a word to either of them—I walked into their room . . . threw everything into suitcases and demoted them to my room on the first floor. . . . I felt guilty but not quite guilty enough not to dispossess them.

KATHARINE HEPBURN

I could be the poster boy for bad judgment.

ROB LOWE

I've got more paternity suits than leisure suits.

ENGELBERT HUMPERDINCK

I am not a good husband or a father. All my daughter sees of me is a different character on a screen.

MARCELLO MASTROIANNI

I've been in trouble most of my life; I've done the most unutterable rubbish, all because of money. I didn't need it . . . the lure of the zeros was simply too great.

RICHARD BURTON

I've put my charm in places that I'm ashamed of . . . and I have at times attracted loyalty on a scale that appalled me, without wishing to do so. I have revelations about myself when I was young and ruthless as somebody who did make indiscriminate use of his seductive powers, not toward women but in work. Somebody who allowed his humanity to be misused.

JOHN LE CARRÉ

Most writers write books that they wouldn't read. I ought to know; I've done it myself.

GORE VIDAL

I work for a government I despise for ends I think criminal.   JOHN MAYNARD KEYNES

To be absolutely honest, what I feel really bad about is that I don't feel worse. That's the ineffectual liberal's problem in a nutshell.

MICHAEL FRAYN

Patton was misunderstood contemporaneously and he's misunderstood here—and I'm ashamed to be a part of it.   GEORGE C. SCOTT

I let down my friends, I let down my country. I let down our system of government.

RICHARD NIXON

Works of art exist to be seen, not talked about, except, perhaps, in their presence. I am thoroughly ashamed of all the babbling about art in which I used to join.   GOETHE

Some of my instincts are reprehensible.

WILLIAM F. BUCKLEY, JR.

I should never be allowed out in private.

RANDOLPH CHURCHILL, apologizing
for his rudeness at a dinner party

I start every morning with the *New York Times*. The first thing I do when I get up is read the obituary column. If my name isn't in it, I get dressed.
ALAN KING

Do you know the first thing I do every day? I read the *New York Times* obituary page, because maybe a pianist has died somewhere.
LEOPOLD GODOWSKY

I always turn to the sports page first. The sports page records people's accomplishments; the front page nothing but man's failure.
EARL WARREN

I read the newspaper avidly. It is my one form of continuous fiction.
ANEURIN BEVAN

When things get too unpleasant, I burn the day's newspaper, pull down the curtains, get out the jugs, and put in a civilized evening.
H. L. MENCKEN

Whenever I get married, I start buying *Gourmet* magazine.   NORA EPHRON

I eat dinner out three hundred sixty nights a year.   WOODY ALLEN

I never travel without my diary. One should always have something sensational to read in the train.   OSCAR WILDE

I always put on a tie when I go out.
                                    GEORGE HAMILTON

Smoking is, if not my life, then at least my hobby. I love to smoke. Smoking is fun. Smoking is cool. Smoking is, as far as I'm concerned, the entire point of being an adult.
                                    FRAN LEBOWITZ

I used to smoke two packs a day and I just hate being a nonsmoker. . . . But I will never consider myself a nonsmoker. Because I always find smokers the most interesting people at the table.   MICHELLE PFEIFFER

It has always been my rule never to smoke when asleep, and never to refrain when awake.   MARK TWAIN

I smoke ten to fifteen cigars a day. At my age, I have to hold onto something.
                                    GEORGE BURNS

I started smoking during the war. I have kept it up ever since. It keeps me healthy.

MARLENE DIETRICH

I know folks all have a tizzy about it, but I like a little bourbon of an evening. It helps me sleep. I don't care much what they say about it.   LILLIAN CARTER

When I was younger, I made it a rule never to take strong drink before lunch. It is now my rule never to do so before breakfast.
                                    WINSTON CHURCHILL

I don't miss booze. I still cause mayhem. I'll always love to frolic, but now I can remember what I've done.   PETER O'TOOLE

Actually, it only takes one drink to get me loaded. Trouble is, I can't remember if it's the thirteenth or the fourteenth.   GEORGE BURNS

Cocaine habit forming? Of course not. I ought to know, I've been using it for years.
                                    TALLULAH BANKHEAD

I've been hooked on everything—dope, drink, sex—but I don't regret any of it. It was fun. I wish I could still do it.   HAROLD ROBBINS

The last thing I swallowed was hair spray. I pulled off the spray top and gulped the ingredients.   KITTY DUKAKIS

The only difference between me and John Belushi is he's dead—and that's just the whim of the gods.　　　RICHARD DREYFUSS

I didn't like illegal drugs, I liked legal drugs . . . I liked medication because I liked the philosophy of it—you're going to feel better when you take two or eight of these, and I always wanted to feel better.　　　CARRIE FISHER

Of course drugs were fun. And that's what's so stupid about anti-drug campaigns: they don't admit that. I can't say I feel particularly scarred or lessened by my experimentation with drugs. They've gotten a very bad name.　　　ANJELICA HUSTON

I don't drink and I don't take drugs. Don't applaud that: If I got shitfaced I'd probably start talking about insurance premiums.
　　　BOBCAT GOLDTHWAITE

I always read the last page of a book first so that if I die before I finish I'll know how it turned out.　　　NORA EPHRON

I'm very careless about objects. That's why I give everything away.　　　JOHN CAGE

Since I am known as a "rich" person, I feel I have to tip at least $5 each time I check my

coat. On top of that, I would have to wear a
very expensive coat, and it would have to be
insured. Added up, without a topcoat I save
over $20,000 a year.   ARISTOTLE ONASSIS

I don't want money. It is only people who pay
their bills who want that, and I never pay
mine.   OSCAR WILDE

I try, each day, to expiate yesterday's guilt.
                          WILLIAM MANCHESTER

I kissed my first woman and smoked my first cigarette on the same day. I have never had time for tobacco since. ARTURO TOSCANINI

I'd the upbringing a nun would envy and that's the truth. Until I was fifteen I was more familiar with Africa than my own body.
JOE ORTON

I left high school a virgin. TOM SELLECK

I've looked on a lot of women with lust. I've committed adultery in my heart many times. This is something God recognizes I will do— and I have done it—and God forgives me for it. JIMMY CARTER

I date men and I date women. What Woody Allen said was true. Say what you will about bisexuality, you have a fifty percent better chance of finding a date on Saturday night.
DAVID GEFFEN

A lot of my peer group think I'm an eccentric bisexual, like I may even have an ammonia-filled tentacle or something somewhere on my body. That's okay.   ROBERT DOWNEY, JR.

> If I had to choose between music and sex, I would pause a long time.
>
> DONALD BARTHELME

I'd rather hit than have sex.   REGGIE JACKSON

> During sex I fantasize that I'm someone else.   RICHARD LEWIS

If I had a cock for a day I would get myself pregnant.   GERMAINE GREER

> We practice safe sex. We gave up the chande-lier a long time ago.   KATHIE LEE GIFFORD

I tried to charm the pants off Bob Dylan, but everyone will be disappointed to learn that I was unsuccessful. I got close—a couple of fast feels in the front seat of a Cadillac.

BETTE MIDLER

> I know there are nights when I have power, when I could put on something and walk in somewhere, and if there is a man who doesn't look at me, it's because he's gay.
>
> KATHLEEN TURNER

No woman has ever slept with me too soon. . . . I've always found promiscuous women interesting. I suspect I would have been promiscuous if I'd been a woman. I certainly have been as a man.   NORMAN MAILER

When I have sex it takes four minutes. And that includes dinner and a show.
GILBERT GOTTFRIED

People called me the guy with the cock in his voice. Maybe that's why in 84 years of life I've been with over 145 women and girls.
RUDY VALLEE

Many, many people have done a lot more sexual experimentation than I have.   ERICA JONG

I don't believe in celibacy—except for myself.   PATRICK MACNEE

Winning a Grammy sure helped me get laid.   BONNIE RAITT

I have to be genuinely in love with a girl to make a pass.   GEORGE CHAKIRIS

If I don't do it every day, I get a headache.
WILLIE NELSON

I can't get to sleep unless I've had a lay.

JOHN F. KENNEDY

I've always gone out with women who swam better than I did. It's as if I were asking them to teach me how to make love. Though I know how to make love (more or less), I have never fully shaken that adolescent boy's insecurity that there was more to it than I could ever imagine, and that I needed a full-time instructress.

PHILLIP LOPATE

I had pretty much always been promiscuous, but right after I started doing *Cheers*, well, I was going on three dates a day. As a guy, you're raised to get as much as you can. Sex, sex, sex, that's what you're after. But after a while, I realized what I was doing was foolhardy. Still, it took some time to travel from the brain . . . groinward. WOODY HARRELSON

I'd like to do a love scene with him just to see what all the yelling is about.

SHIRLEY MACLAINE (of her
brother, Warren Beatty)

I bought a condom and put it in my wallet when I was fourteen. By the time I pulled it out to use it, it was older than the girl I was with. LEWIS GRIZZARD

If I had as many love affairs as I've been given credit for, I'd be in a jar in the Harvard Medical School. FRANK SINATRA

I wish I had as much in bed as I get in the newspapers.　LINDA RONSTADT

The sacrilegious truth is, my sex drive diminished sharply when I started skipping periods, and vanished entirely as soon as they stopped for good. Now the only thing I miss about sex is the cigarette afterward. Next to the first one in the morning, it's the best one of all. It tasted so good that even if I had been frigid I would have pretended otherwise just to be able to smoke it.　FLORENCE KING

The ability to enjoy your sex life is central. I don't give a shit about anything else. My obsession is total. What else is there to live for?　DUDLEY MOORE

I have great respect for someone from a strict Catholic upbringing who can climax without reservation.　ROBERT DOWNEY, JR.

People assume you slept your way to the top. Frankly, I couldn't sleep my way to the middle.　JONI EVANS

Health Matters

If you knew how meat was made, you'd probably lose your lunch. I know—I'm from cattle country. That's why I became a vegetarian.

K. D. LANG

I was raised on pork, and believe me, I'm healthy. TINA TURNER

I won't eat anything that has intelligent life, but I'd gladly eat a network executive or a politician. MARTY FELDMAN

I have no truck with lettuce, cabbage, and similar chlorophyll. Any dietician will tell you that a running foot of apple strudel contains four times the vitamins of a bushel of beans. S. J. PERELMAN

My good health is due to a soup made of white doves. MADAME CHIANG KAI-SHEK

I had a cholesterol test. They found bacon.

BOB ZANY

I take a tremendous amount of vitamins, which includes a giant Swiss pill each morning, and six protein-rich pony pills—what's good for a horse is good for people.

DIANA VREELAND

I once passed a kidney stone during the opening night of a show.

RIP TORN

I have gained and lost the same ten pounds so many times over and over again my cellulite must have déjà vu.

JANE WAGNER

I've been on a constant diet for the last two decades. I've lost a total of 789 pounds. By all accounts, I should be hanging from a charm bracelet.

ERMA BOMBECK

It's pretty sad when a person has to lose weight to play Babe Ruth.

JOHN GOODMAN

The only way you can stay as skinny as I am at my age is to starve.

HELEN GURLEY BROWN

I'm Jewish. I don't work out. If God had intended me to bend over, He'd have put diamonds on the floor.

JOAN RIVERS

I had my nose done and it definitely made me look prettier, but I wouldn't do it again. For about a year, my nose was constantly stuffed up and runny. I had to have it cauterized—which was worse than the surgery—several times. MAUREEN MCGOVERN

I had a couple of screws removed from my leg. The pain actually makes me go a little bit more violent, so I almost enjoy it. BILLY IDOL

I cannot keep myself healthy—too many bad habits deeply ingrained, cardiac bronchitis like the orchestra of death tuning up under water. ANTHONY BURGESS

In spite of chain-smoking Pall Malls since I was fourteen, I think my wind is still good enough for me to go chasing after happiness. KURT VONNEGUT

I enjoy convalescence. It is the part that makes illness worthwhile. GEORGE BERNARD SHAW

I have Bright's disease and he has mine. S. J. PERELMAN

Guilty Pleasures

I do like to see the arms and legs fly.
COLONEL GEORGE S. PATTON III

I actually enjoyed weapons training. I had the eyes to be good at firing the .303 rifle, but not the hands. Yet I relished being instructed on it. And the Bren was such a perfect machine that there was an avid competition to specialize. I never got to the stage of wanting to sleep with one, but I must admit that there were times when, as I eyed the Bren's sleek lines, I discovered in myself a strong urge to fiddle with its gas-escape regulator. CLIVE JAMES

I love watching car races, but if there are no accidents, I'm terribly disappointed. I know people get killed, but I get thrilled to death. GINGER BAKER

I enjoy shopping. It's a kind of hobby to help my nerves. Better than a psychiatrist!
TAMMY FAYE BAKKER

I think the most underrated thing in the world is a good hot bath. With bubbles.

BURT REYNOLDS

Praise shames me, for I secretly beg for it.

RABINDRANATH TAGORE

I can live for two months on a good compliment.

MARK TWAIN

There is no question you get pumped up by the recognition. Then a self-loathing sets in when you realize you're enjoying it.

GEORGE C. SCOTT

I have a sweet tooth for song and music. This is my Polish sin.

POPE JOHN PAUL II

Lawrence [Welk] was not known as the hippest show around. But when nobody was home, I'd tune in.

GREGORY HINES

I never thought my speeches were too long. I enjoyed them.

HUBERT HUMPHREY

I've always been in love with my voice.

ROY ORBISON

I sucked my thumb until I was eleven.

ROSANNA ARQUETTE

When I was really young, I was a voyeur. I trained myself to eavesdrop while looking out the train window and not miss a word. I used to walk around when I was twelve and follow people home. This would even involve taking bus rides with them. I just wanted to see where and how they lived.   MICHAEL HERR

I like seeing my picture in the papers.
JULIE CHRISTIE

I have little patience with anyone who is not self-satisfied. I am always pleased to see my friends, happy to be with my wife and family, but the high spot of every day is when I first catch a glimpse of myself in the shaving mirror.   ROBERT MORLEY

The greatest pleasure when I started making money was not buying cars or yachts but finding myself able to have as many freshly typed drafts as possible.   GORE VIDAL

I love playing bitches.   JOAN CRAWFORD

I'm a caviar freak, though I try not to eat too much of it because of the salt content. But my absolute favorite food is a perfectly ripe white peach. I just love the aroma. Sometimes I'll put some cinnamon on one and pretend it's a pie without the calories.   CRISTINA FERRARE

I . . . go to McDonald's and Burger King on occasion. What else are you going to do when you're on the road and you have to dash in for some food? They are pretty good; they're clean, and you know what you're getting. I don't know why anyone would think I always dine on hummingbirds' tongues or something.　　　　　　　　　　　JULIA CHILD

I like white trash cooking. Cheeseburgers. The greasier the better. Mashed potatoes served in a scoop, a little dent in the top for the gravy. Drake's Devil Dogs for dessert. Pure pleasure; no known nutrient.　　　　ORSON BEAN

It is a rather pleasant experience to be alone in a bank at night.　　　　WILLIE SUTTON

This may sound terribly selfish, but I love the freedom that I have. I don't have to worry about anybody but myself, I don't have to worry about a man's wardrobe, or his relatives, or his schedule, or his menu, or his allergies. I would not be married again.　ANN LANDERS

I invariably check the medicine cabinet if I use the bathroom in someone else's house; in a small apartment where there is no guest loo, entire medical, social and sexual histories can be constructed from the specific.
　　　　　　　　JOHN GREGORY DUNNE

I have never killed a man, but I have read
many obituaries with a lot of pleasure.

CLARENCE DARROW

I like the moment when I break a man's ego.

BOBBY FISCHER

I sometimes feel that I'm impersonating the
dark unconscious of the human race. I know
this sounds sick, but I love it. VINCENT PRICE

I'd never tell anybody this, but I have *Wood-
stock* on tape—just for the clichéd language.
Like Arlo Guthrie saying, "Can you dig it,
man?" It's a riot.   GARY SHANDLING

I completed the course work for the M.A. but
did not finish my thesis because I found something better to do. I spent the entire spring
semester writing stories for the true confessions magazines. After turning out footnoted
reams on such pressing topics as the annex-
ation of Schleswig-Holstein and the reign of
Pippin the Short, I got five cents a word for "I
Committed Adultery in a Diabetic Coma" and
it felt *great*. I had thrown off the vague guilt of
the welfare scholar and become a productive
member of society at last.   FLORENCE KING

All the things I like to do are either immoral,
illegal or fattening. ALEXANDER WOOLLCOTT

WOLFGANG AMADEUS MOZART
Dirty Jokes

14–16th November, 1777.

I, johannes Chrisostomus Amadeus Wolfgangus sigismundus Mozart, confess my fault in that the day before yesterday, and yesterday (and on many previous occasions), I did not come home till twelve o'clock at night; and that from ten o'clock until the hour aforenamed at Canabich's house, in the presence of, and in company with, Canabich, his wife and daughter, Herr Schazmeister, Ramm and Lang, I frequently—not gravely but quite frivolously—made verses; and those obscene ones, about dung, excrement and *arschlecken*, in thought and word— but not in deed. But I should not have behaved so impiously if the ring-leader, that is to say Lisel (Elizabetha Canabich), had not urged me on and encouraged me to it so lustily; and I must admit that I enjoyed it prodigiously. I confess all these my sins and transgressions from the bottom of my heart, and in the hope of confessing them more often, I am firmly resolved constantly to *improve* on the evil manner of life which I have begun.

Therefore I beg for holy dispensation, if it can be managed; and if not, it's all one to me, for the game will go on all the same.

Predilections

I am attracted to thin, tall, good-looking men who have one common denominator. They must be lurking bastards. EDNA O'BRIEN

I go for tough, uncommunicative guys who ride motorcycles. ALLY SHEEDY

I'm always attracted to the wrong kind of guy—like the pope. CAROL LEIFER

I've always found insects exciting. LUIS BUÑUEL

I like, roughly in the order described: (1) God, (2) my family and friends, (3) my country, (4) J. S. Bach, (5) peanut butter, and (6) good English prose. WILLIAM F. BUCKLEY, JR.

I love Mexican food, Southern Gothic writers, horror movies, fireplaces, corn on the cob,

Dr Pepper, old movies, and ketchup on my steak.   REX REED

> I only ask for three things out of life, maybe four: to be out of jail; to eat regular; to get a little love at home; and maybe a little on the outside.   CARL SANDBURG

I prefer girls who are young. When I eat a peach, I don't want it overripe. I want that peach when it's peaking.   JIM BROWN

> I am more attracted by beautiful details—the mouth, the nose—than by the whole. Finding myself in front of a beauty can be frightening. A beautiful woman whom you love is always a danger for you. You are always afraid that someone will take her away from you. I much prefer a nonbeauty with a great personality.   GIORGIO ARMANI

I get hit on all the time by gay women. I'm flattered that they like me . . . but I am not gay. I have a gay following because I love and understand gay people. My dearest friends are gay men. . . . What people do behind their closed doors is certainly not my concern unless I'm behind there with 'em and wantin' to do whatever. I grew up around macho men and have had lovers that are that macho type. I'm kinda drawn to that for my lovers for the most part.   DOLLY PARTON

I sleep with men and with women. I am neither queer nor not queer, nor am I bisexual.   ALLEN GINSBERG

Only love interests me, and I am only in contact with things that revolve around love.
                                  MARC CHAGALL

What I tend to go for, and what interests me, is not the hero but the coward . . . not the success, but the failure.   JOHN SCHLESINGER

I love Virginians because Virginians are all snobs and I like snobs. A snob has to spend so much time being a snob that he has little time left to meddle with you.
                              WILLIAM FAULKNER

I get a kick out of movie stars.
                                JACK NICHOLSON

My hates have always occupied my mind much more actively and have given greater spiritual satisfaction than my friendships.
                              WESTBROOK PEGLER

I always had a tremendous interest in big tits.   RUSS MEYER

I have always loved backs.   PHILLIP LOPATE

I don't write polite letters. I don't like to plea-bargain. I like to fight.   ROY COHN

I've never stayed in one place long. I worked a lot of sit-down jobs in the early days out of necessity, but I was always wishing that Hank Thompson or one of those big bands would hire me so I could step onto the bus with them . . . and I've never wanted to get off since.

WILLIE NELSON

I've tried everything but coprophagia and necrophilia, and I like kissing best.

JOHN WATERS

I am not a cat man, but a dog man.

JAMES THURBER

I prefer cats to dogs because they are not so loud and clumsy, or so overtly masculine. They have a feminine grace.   A. L. ROWSE

I've never been a fan of personality-conflict burgers and identity-crisis omelets with patchouli oil. I function very well on a diet that consists of Chicken Catastrophe and Eggs Overwhelming and a tall, cool Janitor-in-a-Drum. I like to walk out of a restaurant with enough gas to open a Mobil station.

TOM WAITS

Having to choose between the White House and the penitentiary, I'd choose the penitentiary. WILLIAM TECUMSEH SHERMAN

In politics it is necessary to betray one's country or the electorate. I prefer to betray the electorate. CHARLES DE GAULLE

I prefer the word *homemaker*, because *housewife* always implies that there may be a wife someplace else. BELLA ABZUG

Now, nature, as I am only too well aware, has her enthusiasts, but on the whole, I am not to be counted among them. To put it rather bluntly, I am not the type who wants to go back to the land; I am the type who wants to go back to the hotel. FRAN LEBOWITZ

I like persons better than principles and I like persons with no principles better than anything else in the world. OSCAR WILDE

I prefer the wicked rather than the foolish. The wicked sometimes rest. ALEXANDRE DUMAS

I'd much rather play with a poor loser than any kind of winner. BRIAN DONLEVY

I prefer neurotic people. I like to hear rumblings beneath the surface.

STEPHEN SONDHEIM

I can't type; but if I could type, I'd rather play the harpsichord. PETER USTINOV

I'm tired of love: I'm still more tired of rhyme.
But money gives me pleasure all the time.

HILAIRE BELLOC

I would sooner read a timetable or a catalogue than nothing at all. W. SOMERSET MAUGHAM

I read books like mad, but I am careful not to let anything I read influence me.

MICHAEL CAINE

I don't have anything against wine, but I do admire the distilled grains. MICHAEL HERR

I can't stand light. I hate weather. My idea of heaven is moving from one smoke-filled room to another. PETER O'TOOLE

If I had the choice between smoked salmon and tinned salmon, I'd have it tinned. With vinegar. HAROLD WILSON

I would rather be first in a small village in
Gaul than second in command in Rome.

JULIUS CAESAR

I'd rather be called sleazy than to be identified
as intelligent.   PHIL DONAHUE

I'd rather direct than produce. Any day. And
twice on Sunday.   STEVEN SPIELBERG

I'd rather be a great bad poet than a good bad
poet.   OGDEN NASH

I'd rather kill a man than a snake. Not because
I love snakes or hate men. It is a question,
rather, of proportion.   EDWARD ABBEY

I had rather be shut up in a very modest cottage, with my books, my family and a few old
friends, dining on simple bacon, and letting
the world roll on as it liked, than to occupy
the most splendid post which any human
power can give.   THOMAS JEFFERSON

I'd much rather sit next to a smoker in a restaurant than a nose blower.   LEWIS GRIZZARD

I'd rather be dead than singing "Satisfaction"
when I'm forty-five.   MICK JAGGER

I'd rather ride down the street on a camel than give what is sometimes called an in-depth interview. I'd rather ride down the street on a camel nude. In a snowstorm. Backward.

WARREN BEATTY

I'd rather wake up in the middle of nowhere than in any city on earth.   STEVE MCQUEEN

I would rather lie on a sofa than sweep beneath it.   SHIRLEY CONRAN

If I had to choose, I would rather have birds than airplanes.   CHARLES A. LINDBERGH

I never eat when I can dine.   MAURICE CHEVALIER

As far as I'm concerned, the best place in the world to be is on a good cutting horse working cattle.   SANDRA DAY O'CONNOR

Minks are mean little critters. Vicious, horrible little animals who eat their own. They're not beavers. I wouldn't wear beavers. I'd rather have a mink coat made of mean little critters that are killed in a very nice way and treated nicely for their short mean lives, so that I could be kept warm.   VALERIE PERRINE

Suspicions Confirmed

There used to be a me, but I had it surgically removed. PETER SELLERS

I never read very much. STEVEN SPIELBERG

I own and operate a ferocious ego. BILL MOYERS

I never had a date in high school or in college. SALLY JESSY RAPHAEL

I led a very sheltered life. I had never seen a man hit his wife. I had never seen any drunkenness. I had never seen any poverty. I knew these things were happening, but they never happened to me. ANN LANDERS

I've always looked better lying down. JERRY HALL

I am naturally suspicious of deep thinkers in relation to motion pictures.

DARRYL F. ZANUCK

I would rather take a fifty-mile hike than crawl through a book. I prefer to skip the long ones and get a synopsis from the story department.

JACK L. WARNER

I don't know my own telephone number.

AXL ROSE

I grew up wanting to be Nelson Riddle.

BARRY MANILOW

Success didn't spoil me; I've always been insufferable.

FRAN LEBOWITZ

I've run more risks eating my way across the country than in all my driving.

DUNCAN HINES

I'll spend $50,000 on traveling, but I won't spend $200 on clothes.

JODIE FOSTER

I'm not a lovable man. RICHARD NIXON

I'm not smart enough to lie. RONALD REAGAN

Startling Revelations

It often happens that I wake at night and begin to think about a serious problem and decide I must tell the pope about it. Then I wake up completely and remember that I *am* the pope. POPE JOHN XXIII

I have always hated that damn James Bond. I'd like to kill him. SEAN CONNERY

I don't actually have a vivid imagination. FREDERICK FORSYTH

Sometimes when I sit down to practice and there is no one else in the room, I have to stifle an impulse to ring for the elevator man and offer him money to come in and hear me. ARTHUR RUBINSTEIN

People think I sit here and push buttons and get things accomplished. Well, I spent today kissing behinds. HARRY S. TRUMAN

I bit the head off a live bat the other night. It
was like eating a Crunchie wrapped in cham-
ois leather.   OZZY OSBORNE

I *hate* to paint portraits! I hope never to paint
another portrait in my life.

JOHN SINGER SARGENT

I derive no pleasure from the process of
directing.   FRANCIS COPPOLA

Nothing induces me to read a novel except
when I have to make money by writing about
it. I detest them.   VIRGINIA WOOLF

I get tired immediately upon entering a
museum.   LOUIS KAHN

There are times when I think that the reading
I have done in the past has had no effect except to cloud my mind and make me indecisive.   ROBERTSON DAVIES

I've never been in love, and as far as I know
no one has ever been in love with me.

QUENTIN CRISP

I made my mistakes, but in all my years of
public life I have never profited from public
service. I have earned every cent.

RICHARD NIXON

I thought he was a very nice gentleman. . . . I thought so right up to the moment I cut his throat.   PERRY SMITH

I am hopeless on discussing style and technique. I don't even know where the volume is. I was in a music store and this guy came up to me and asked what kind of guitar strings I used. I just told him long, shiny silver things.   PAUL MCCARTNEY

I can't play guitar and sing at the same time. My brain can't handle it. I can't even play rhythm guitar and sing. It's hard enough for me to stay in tune just *singing*.
                                 FRANK ZAPPA

Composers often tell you that they don't read criticisms of their works. . . . I am an exception. I admit to a curiosity about the slightest clue as to the meaning of a piece of mine—a meaning, that is, other than the one I know I have put there.   AARON COPLAND

The real, native, South Seas food is lousy. You can't eat it.
    VICTOR J. ("TRADER VIC") BERGERON

I don't much enjoy looking at paintings in general. I know too much about them. I take them apart.   GEORGIA O'KEEFE

In the early days of the December that my father was to die, my younger brother brought me the news that I was a Jew. I was then a transplanted Englishman in America, married, with one son and, though unconsoled by any religion, a nonbelieving member of two Christian churches. On hearing the tidings, I was pleased to find that I was pleased.

CHRISTOPHER HITCHENS

I have had my television aerials removed. It's the moral equivalent of a prostate operation.

MALCOLM MUGGERIDGE

When I got my first television set, I stopped caring so much about having close relationships.

ANDY WARHOL

When we got into office, the thing that surprised me most was to find that things were just as bad as we'd been saying they were.

JOHN F. KENNEDY

I don't care what is written about me so long as it isn't true.

KATHARINE HEPBURN

I was thirty-two when I started cooking; up until then, I just ate.

JULIA CHILD

People assume you can't be shy and be on television. They're wrong.

DIANE SAWYER

I have only ever read one book in my life, and that is *White Fang*. It's so frightfully good I've never bothered to read another.

NANCY MITFORD

I think I may boast myself to be, with all possible vanity, the most unlearned and uninformed female who ever dared to be an authoress.

JANE AUSTEN

I understand women. All I know is women. I'm surprised I didn't grow up to be a transvestite.

ARSENIO HALL

I know how it feels to be a woman because I *am* a woman. And I won't be satisfied as just a man.

PETE TOWNSHEND

OK, I've experimented with both sexes, but I'm not a limp-wristed floozy and I'm not a transvestite. I'm a very masculine person.

BOY GEORGE

I've never seen *Leave It to Beaver* and I've never seen an *I Love Lucy* all the way through.

HARRY SHEARER

I fasted one time for six days just on water, marijuana and headphones.

STERLING HAYDEN

My mother is terrified that I'll get married before I sow my wild oats.   MOLLY RINGWALD

When I was a teenager in Houston, it really did seem that country music was all middle-aged men singing about cheating on their wives and drinking. Of course, at seventeen you wonder how anyone over thirty breathes on their own.   K. T. OSLIN

If I had it to do over, I would go through puberty again, but I would do it where no one could see me.   ROY BLOUNT, JR.

I guess this means that now I can buy my own house and own my own recording studio.   TIFFANY, upon turning eighteen

When I was eighteen years old, and did look perfect, I was so insecure that when I was in elevators, I would face the wall because I thought the lighting was so bad.

CYBILL SHEPHERD

At the age of twenty-two I believed myself to be unextinguishable.   SIEGFRIED SASSOON

I was never an Angry Young Man. I am angry only when I hit my thumb with a hammer.

KINGSLEY AMIS

I shall never be as old as I was between twenty and thirty.   V. S. PRITCHETT

I am past thirty, and three parts iced over.

MATTHEW ARNOLD

I'll be dead by the time I'm forty.

ROD STEWART

I am resolved to grow fat and look young till forty, and then slip out of the world with the first wrinkle and the reputation of five-and-twenty.   JOHN DRYDEN

When I turned forty . . . friends warned me not to admit my real age, but I thought they were ridiculous. I'm a good example of what a forty-year-old woman should look like.

VICTORIA PRINCIPAL

I'm forty years old but, damn, I'm still good-looking. BRUCE SPRINGSTEEN

At sixteen I was stupid, confused, insecure and indecisive. At twenty-five I was wise, self-confident, prepossessing and assertive. At forty-five I am stupid, confused, insecure and indecisive. Who would have supposed that maturity is only a short break in adolescence?   JULES FEIFFER

I'm always asked, "What about being too old to rock and roll?" Presumably lots of writers get better as they get older. So why shouldn't I?   LOU REED

I'm at the age where food has taken the place of sex in my life. In fact, I've just had a mirror put over my kitchen table.
                                    RODNEY DANGERFIELD

Growing older, I have lost the need to be political, which means, in this country, the need to be left. I am driven into grudging toleration of the Conservative Party because it is the party of non-politics, of resistance to politics.   KINGSLEY AMIS

I have everything I had twenty years ago—except now it's all lower.   GYPSY ROSE LEE

I don't plan to grow old gracefully. I plan to have face-lifts until my ears meet.
                                    RITA RUDNER

I used to dread getting older because I thought I would not be able to do all the things I wanted to do, but now that I am older I find that I don't want to do them. NANCY ASTOR

When I was young, I was told: "You'll see, when you're fifty." I'm fifty and I haven't seen a thing. ERIK SATIE

This is what fifty looks like. GLORIA STEINEM

I have now turned fifty and am going through menopause and I enjoy a little litigation. It's costly, perhaps, but salutary, and considerably less expensive than keeping racehorses or getting married. GORE VIDAL

I had the menopause. I never liked being a woman, I never liked having to be feminine, although I could do a pretty good imitation of it. But once you go through the menopause, you get your true personality back.

FLORENCE KING

I refuse to admit that I am more than fifty-two, even if that does make my sons illegitimate. NANCY ASTOR

I've had my day as a leading man. I'm not fighting tooth and claw to get back to the top

of the heap. I am quite happy in the fullness
of my years.   GREGORY PECK

My signature is holding up but sometimes I
almost forget what my name is. I look down as
I sign and I think, Is that right? Is this me?
      LAUREN BACALL

Retirement at sixty-five is ridiculous. When I
was sixty-five I still had pimples.
      GEORGE BURNS

I'll never make the mistake of turning seventy
again.   CASEY STENGEL

If I had any decency, I'd be dead. Most of my
friends are.   DOROTHY PARKER

I don't have a warm personal enemy left.
They've all died off. I miss them terribly because they've helped define me.
      CLARE BOOTHE LUCE

When one has reached eighty-one one likes to
sit back and let the world turn by itself, without trying to push it.   SEAN O'CASEY

When my time comes, just skin me and put
me right up there on Trigger, just as if nothing
had ever changed.   ROY ROGERS

I have always thought that a woman has the right to treat the subject of her age with ambiguity until, perhaps, she passes into the realm of over ninety. Then it is better she be candid with herself and with the world.

HELENA RUBINSTEIN

I remember my youth and the feeling that will never come back any more—the feeling that I could last forever, outlast the sea, the earth, and all men; the deceitful feeling that lures us on to joys, to perils, to love, to vain effort—to death; the triumphant conviction of strength, the heart of life in the handful of dust, the glow in the heart that with every year grows dim, grows cold, grows small, and expires—and expires, too soon, too soon—before life itself.

JOSEPH CONRAD

JACKIE COOPER
Normal Urges

For a boy like me, with very normal urges, Hollywood and the movie studios were a spectacular place to grow up. For example, when I was sixteen, and at Paramount, one of us kids discovered the Paulette Goddard scenic view. Pretty soon we all knew about it. Somebody had noticed that there was a vantage point with a direct, unimpeded, and total view into her dressing room. Furthermore—and this was the juicy part—Miss Goddard liked to loll around her dressing room topless.

You can imagine what sport a bunch of young teenage boys would have with that knowledge. Paulette Goddard was a lady of fantastic construction. I cannot vouch for my contemporaries, for Mickey Rooney and Jackie Searle and the others, but I know that I would find many excuses to take myself to that particular vantage point and just hope that she was there and in her usual state of astounding undress.

On any lot, too, there was a constant parade of chorus girls and dress (or undress) extras, for the lavish musicals and spectacular costume dramas that were being filmed there. Just a stroll around the lot, and an enterprising young lad could gawk at dozens of gorgeous girls, and since this particular enterprising young lad was well known, they gawked back. I was no longer in the cute and precious stage, so they had no excuse to fondle me, but I was a star, and they were almost always ambitious, so they would talk to me, and I quickly learned how to converse with girls.

I remember one day when I was eleven or twelve, on the MGM lot, watching with tremendous interest the progress of Jean Harlow down a street. She was wearing a gown so sheer that it was possible—indeed, probable—that everything she had was in almost plain view. And she had plenty. My mother was with me, and she noticed my interest, and she laughed. She didn't reprimand me for gawking, and she wasn't embarrassed or shocked by it. She thought it was normal and an indication that I was normal and, also, growing up.

I knew the facts of life. My mother was a very progressive and intelligent lady, and she had answered all my childhood and adolescent questions fully and without embarrassment. If she was, for example, talking to a friend about "labor" when I was nine or ten, and I would ask her what she meant, she would tell me. No hesitation and no detours. Yet she would never give me too much information. Some parents I know, in their desire to be forward-thinking, will answer a child's innocent question with an hour-long dissertation complete with slides. At that age, if I saw a pregnant lady and I asked my mother why she had such a fat tummy, my mother would say, "She's carrying a baby in her stomach." I would say, "Oh," and that would be that. No more, no less. My curiosity would be amply satisfied, but I would not be burdened with information which I did not need and could not, for that matter, understand yet.

My mother answered all my questions, and she would always give another bit of helpful information. She would caution me not to talk to the other kids about such matters. I guess she felt that they would give me the wrong dope—kids often having been given wrong ideas by other kids—which would only confuse me. I never did ask the other kids.

In my era the human body was pretty much a hidden commodity. Until Paulette Goddard's time I really had only seen one body—mine. There were no centerfolds in magazines for kids to moon over. The bikini hadn't been invented yet. There were no nude scenes in movies. And so girls, to me as I entered those exciting teenage years, were still a mystery. What was it they had, under all those clothes, which somehow stirred me? I knew, of course, and yet I didn't know. I knew intellectually, but I had yet to see for myself.

There had been one small experience when I was very young. It had been when I was so young, in fact, that it served only to disturb me rather than excite me.

When I was seven or eight, we rented a beach house. This particular beach house had an outdoor shower. My aunt Julie—a year or so younger than my mother and the one with the family reputation of being the beauty—would get in the shower with me. It was an enclosed shower, so nobody else could see or even knew. We were both naked. I remember looking at her. I remember being bothered by it. Nothing happened in the shower, but it was, to me, an unpleasant experience.

I was twelve or so when I went to some parties when we lived in Ocean Park. There was a little girl across the street whose name, if my memory isn't playing tricks on me, was Farrell Minick. She was the first girl of twelve or thirteen—the first *big* girl—who paid any attention to me, the kind of attention a boy realizes comes because he is liked, not because he has a worm in his pocket. There were parties, and we went, and we played spin the bottle. My first real kiss was from Farrell Minick after the bottle had spun in her direction.

I was seventeen, and I began to go over to Joan Crawford's house to play badminton. She was a friend of my mother's and, over the years, had offered me the use of her court. She didn't have room for a tennis court, so had put in a badminton court, and I had learned to enjoy playing that game.

The court was right off the pool house, and one day, sweaty from an hour of exertion, I went into the pool house with Joan. I was thirsty and she poured me a Coke. As she bent over, I looked down her dress.

"You're growing up, aren't you?" she said.

I was brash, fresh from some romantic triumph, I suppose, and I made some remark which I assumed was sophisticated, witty, and very sexually provocative.

"You had better get out of here, young man," she said.

But I didn't go. Instead, I made a move toward her, and she stood up, looked at me appraisingly, and then closed all the drapes. And I made love to Joan Crawford. Or, rather, she made love to me.

Over the next six months or so the performance was repeated eight or nine times. After the first time, however, it was always late at night. I would set a date with her, then manage to sneak out of the house after my mother and stepfather had gone to sleep. I would roll my car down the street until I was far enough away so I could start the engine without waking them. And I would drive to Joan's house.

She was a very erudite professor of love. At the time I suppose she was in her early thirties. I was seventeen. She was a wild woman. She would bathe me, powder me, cologne me. Then she would do it over again. She would put on high heels, a garter belt, and a large hat and pose in front of the mirror, turning this way and that way.

"Look," she would say. I was already looking. But that sort of thing didn't particularly excite me. I kept thinking: The lady is crazy.

But I recognized that she was an extraordinary performer, that I was learning things that most men don't learn until they are much older—if at all. There was never any drinking or drugs with her. It was all business. She was very organized. When I left, she would put me on her calendar for the next visit. I could hardly wait.

One night, after one of our sessions, she said that was the last time. She said I should never call her again.

"And put it all out of your mind," she said. "It never happened."

And then she gave me one last kiss and added, "But we'll always be friends."

I was floating during that period. Fortunately I had enough sense not to blab my conquest all over town, but it was a magnificent secret to have. My friends might brag about some pimply-faced teenager or gawky sixteen-year-old they had had, and I would nod my congratulations. And I would think to myself: But I have been with one of the Love

Goddesses of the Screen. Maybe I didn't say anything because I had enough sense not to. But maybe it was because I knew they wouldn't have believed me.

The last time I saw Joan Crawford was when I was doing a guest shot in Peter Falk's *Columbo* series. She was on the Universal lot at the same time, doing something, and the studio was buzzing with the news that Crawford was around. By accident, I happened to run into her, and she took my hand, looked into my eyes, and, I think, remembered.

Tough Talk

I captured some of the people who tried to assassinate me. I ate them before they ate me.

IDI AMIN

I'm not the type to get ulcers. I give them.

ED KOCH

I don't want any yes-men around me. I want everybody to tell me the truth even if it costs them their jobs.

SAMUEL GOLDWYN

I don't meet the competition, I crush it.

CHARLES REVSON

I would walk over my grandmother if necessary to get Nixon re-elected.

CHARLES COLSON

My message to men is: "Don't screw around with women because they can turn around and screw you back."

JACKIE COLLINS

200—True Confessions

When I sing, people shut up.

BARBRA STREISAND

I'm as confident as Cleopatra's pussy.

BETTE MIDLER

I do unto others what they do unto me, only worse.

JIMMY HOFFA

If people screw me, I screw back in spades.

DONALD TRUMP

Just because you like my stuff doesn't mean I owe you anything.

BOB DYLAN

I'm nobody's kid sister.

PRINCESS LEE RADZIWILL

I leave before being left. *I* decide.

BRIGITTE BARDOT

When I go, I'll take New Year's Eve with me.

GUY LOMBARDO

I could spit in the mythological eye of the media every morning. They would still love me.

NORMAN MAILER

When I split an infinitive, God damn it, I split it so it stays split.

RAYMOND CHANDLER

Get in my way when I really want to accomplish
something, I can be a mean mother.

DICK CLARK

I've got a right to knock down anybody holding a bat.   EARLY WYNN

If you start throwing hedgehogs under me I
shall throw two porcupines under you.
                              NIKITA KHRUSHCHEV

When the last dime is gone, I'll sit on the curb
outside with a pencil and a ten-cent notebook
and start the whole thing over again.
                              PRESTON STURGES

I'll dispose of my teeth as I think fit and after
they've gone I'll get along. I started off living
on gruel, and by God, I can always go back to
it again.   S. J. PERELMAN

I believe that if I ever had to practice cannibal-
ism, I might manage it if there were enough
tarragon around.   JAMES BEARD

I've been through it all, baby. I'm Mother
Courage.   ELIZABETH TAYLOR

Frankly, I don't mind not being president, I just mind that someone else is.

EDWARD M. KENNEDY

I don't believe I'll ever get credit for anything I do in foreign affairs, no matter how successful it is, because I didn't go to Harvard.

LYNDON BAINES JOHNSON

I have tried to lift France out of the mud. But she will return to her errors and vomitings. I cannot prevent the French from being French.

CHARLES DE GAULLE

Most leading men can't be supportive of my work because they're too concerned about themselves. Or their penises.

SEAN YOUNG

I was too independent for Mick [Jagger]. I wasn't proper enough for him. He's a chauvinist.

ANITA PALLENBERG

I'm glad I didn't have a piece of *The Exorcist*.
I'd feel stupid to be a millionaire and still
work, and I wouldn't know what to do if I
didn't work.   ELLEN BURSTYN

I don't do Shakespeare. I don't talk in that
kind of broken English.   MR. T

Acting is not my language at all.
                    MIKHAIL BARYSHNIKOV

All they ever did for me at MGM was change
my leading men and the water in my pool.
                         ESTHER WILLIAMS

If I'd had breasts I'd have ruled the world.
                           JULIE HARRIS

If God had given me Burt Bacharach's per-
sona—the hair, the piano—I would have de-
stroyed the world.   SAMMY CAHN

I would have liked a bigger career. I would
have liked to be a major star. . . . I felt an enormous rivalry with Paul, although I wouldn't
admit it to myself. In truth, I was always uncomfortable that Paul was so much bigger than
I was. Uncomfortable and even angry because
he was living my fantasy, being what I had
always wanted to be: a star.
                     JOANNE WOODWARD

I've been in one place for too long. I'm sitting here in Los Angeles getting soft. Twenty-seven years old, balding and without a shred of inspiration; petting my cat, thinking about exercise, never reading a good script. I haven't even had a decent dream in months.

NICOLAS CAGE

It's a drag having to wear socks during matches, because the tan, like, stops at the ankles. I can never get my skin, like, color-coordinated.

MONICA SELES

I don't know what to do or where to turn on this taxation matter. Somewhere there must be a book that tells about it, where I could go to straighten it out in my mind. But I don't know where the book is, and maybe I couldn't read it if I found it. My God, this is a hell of a place for a man like me to be!

WARREN G. HARDING

You get a little stir crazy during the week.
RONALD REAGAN, on living
in the White House

If I'm such a legend, then why am I so lonely?
If I'm such a legend, then why do I sit at home
for hours staring at the damned telephone,
hoping it's out of order, even calling the opera-
tor asking her if she's sure it's not out of order?
Let me tell you legends are all very well if
you've got somebody around who loves you,
some man who's not afraid to be in love with
Judy Garland.   JUDY GARLAND

I'm sick of carrying guns and beating up
women.   JAMES CAGNEY

I find all this money a considerable burden.
J. PAUL GETTY

I can't afford to bulge. Being a sixty-four-year-
old sex symbol is a hell of a weight to
carry.   JOHN FORSYTHE

Being a sex symbol is a heavy load to carry,
especially when one is tired, hurt and be-
wildered.   MARILYN MONROE

People have been so busy relating to how I
look, it's a miracle I didn't become a self-conscious blob of protoplasm.   ROBERT REDFORD

I'm all mixed up and I can't keep up with everything that's happening.   ELVIS PRESLEY

The worst part about being me is when people want me to make them laugh.   JACK LEMMON

I feel like a hard hat a lot of the time. I feel like I'm sixty floors up and people are dropping rivets on my head. I don't want to be a mogul. I want to be a director.
                              STEVEN SPIELBERG

When *Animal House* turned out the way it did, they all rushed to me with barrels of money begging me to make them rich.
                                   JOHN LANDIS

I am a typed director. If I made *Cinderella*, the audience would immediately be looking for a body in the coach.   ALFRED HITCHCOCK

My whole life is a movie. It's just that there are no dissolves. I have to live every agonizing moment of it. My life needs editing.
                                    MORT SAHL

In a restaurant or at a function I just walk straight in and it's an eternity. When I'm sitting, it's OK, but then I have to start thinking of a shortcut out.   SOPHIA LOREN

Sometimes I've been to a party where no one spoke to me a whole evening. The men, frightened by their wives or sweeties, would give me a wide berth. And the ladies would gang up in a corner to discuss my dangerous character.　MARILYN MONROE

I don't like to be bugged in bathrooms. I mean, people hand me cassettes under the stall. It's brutal.　BONNIE RAITT

All I have to do is pose for a picture and I'm getting married to the person standing next to me.　STEVEN SPIELBERG

I arise in the morning torn between a desire to improve (or save) the world and a desire to enjoy (or savor) the world. This makes it hard to plan the day.　E. B. WHITE

I get up in the morning, spend the day working, and watch a lot of bad television. That's about it, except that I have a number of guests around. People with guns.　SALMAN RUSHDIE

Some mornings it just doesn't seem worth it to gnaw through the leather straps.　EMO PHILIPS

Sometimes when you have everything, you can't really tell what matters.　CHRISTINA ONASSIS

It really costs me a lot emotionally to watch myself on-screen. I think of myself—and feel—like I'm quite young, and then I look at this old man with the baggy chins and the tired eyes and the receding hairline and all that.

GENE HACKMAN

It's a full-time job just trying to decide how to spend all this money.   ARTHUR C. CLARKE

I get fifteen or twenty letters a day for everything from Yugoslavian dog illnesses to marathon diseases. It numbs you. . . . So you write off a check for twenty dollars to a charity to absolve yourself of guilt.   ANJELICA HUSTON

Just standing around looking beautiful is so boring, really boring, so boring.

MICHELLE PFEIFFER

I would like to be Maria, but there is La Callas who demands that I carry myself with her dignity.   MARIA CALLAS

Nobody can be exactly like me. Sometimes even I have trouble doing it.

TALLULAH BANKHEAD

I've never looked through a keyhole without finding someone was looking back.

JUDY GARLAND

When I'm writing songs, the minutes are like hours. I sit there with nothing but a big picture of Greil Marcus in my head hanging over the piano. RANDY NEWMAN

Sometimes I feel like a figment of my own imagination. LILY TOMLIN

Sometimes I feel like an old hooker. CHER

When I go to the beauty parlor, I always use the emergency entrance. Sometimes I just go for an estimate. PHYLLIS DILLER

It's tough to find a secure black man who doesn't feel threatened that your career might serve to deball him. DIAHANN CARROLL

In the eyes of the police I'm more than just famous. I'm big, black and arrogant. There are cops in L.A. who would love to send me to San Quentin for 49,000 years. JIM BROWN

If I would believe what I read about myself, I would hate my guts too. ZSA ZSA GABOR

It's confusing. I've had so many wives and so many children I don't know which house to go to first on Christmas. MICKEY ROONEY

I Can't Live Like This—211

One makes sacrifices to be Superwoman. I gave birth to a child who has so much energy. I sometimes ask myself, Why would God give this child more energy than He gave me when I have to take care of him and then take care of Ryan? FARRAH FAWCETT

In my heart I feel Mexican–German. I feel if I were to organize it correctly, I would try to sing like a Mexican and think like a German. I get it mixed up sometimes anyway. I sing like a Nazi and think like a Mexican and I can't get anything right. LINDA RONSTADT

What everybody sees is this big glamour life, but you don't appreciate things as much anymore. You don't appreciate that fancy car like you would if you had to work twice as hard to get it. So the money is not as big a deal as you think. You know what I'm saying? VANILLA ICE

I have never been able to do anything that was accepted straight off. MARCEL DUCHAMP

I don't even get an allowance. MACAULAY CULKIN

I can see the humorous side of things and enjoy the fun when it comes; but look where I will, there seems to me always more sadness than joy in my life. JEROME K. JEROME

It's hard to drink as much bourbon as I do and
be an actor.   GEORGE PEPPARD

Every time I paint a portrait I lose a friend.
                              JOHN SINGER SARGENT

First I lost my weight, then I lost my voice,
and now I lost Onassis.   MARIA CALLAS

It's all happening too fast. I've got to put the
brakes on or I'll smack into something.
                                    MEL GIBSON

I've worked like a dog all my life, honey.
Dancing, as Fred Astaire said, is next to ditch
digging. You sweat and you slave and the audience doesn't think you have a brain in your
head.   ANN MILLER

I live each day under a threat of death. I know
that I can meet a violent end.
                          MARTIN LUTHER KING, JR.

To me happiness is when I am merely miserable and not suicidal.   BOB FOSSE

They have vilified me, they have crucified me,
yes, they have even criticized me.
                              RICHARD J. DALEY

How I Did It

To get them to like you, I figured you sort of had to be their ideal. I don't mean a handsome knight riding a white horse, but a fellow who answered the description of a right guy.

GARY COOPER

I'm not a genetically superior person. I built my body. SYLVESTER STALLONE

When I played drunks I had to remain sober because I didn't know how to play them when I was drunk. RICHARD BURTON

Like an old Model-T Ford, I had to be cranked up. MARIE DRESSLER

I grew a beard for Nero, in *Quo Vadis*, but Metro-Goldwyn-Mayer thought it didn't look real, so I had to wear a false one.

PETER USTINOV

I made films that I would like to have seen
when I was a young man.

FRANÇOIS TRUFFAUT

I completely storyboarded *The Maltese Falcon*
because I didn't want to lose face with the
crew. I wanted to give the impression that I
knew what I was doing. JOHN HUSTON

I kept the same suit for six years—and the
same dialogue. We just changed the title of the
picture and the leading lady.

ROBERT MITCHUM

At first, I wanted to be a model, but they told
me I was too flat-chested. So I went to Wool-
worth's for a special bra, stuffed some cotton
into it and went back a few weeks later. I got
the job—twenty-five dollars a week.

LEONA HELMSLEY

Ivana [Trump] and I are friends, but we're very
different. She married a rich man. I earned everything I have. EVA GABOR

I needed the good will of the legislature of four
states. I "formed" the legislative bodies with
my own money. I found that it was cheaper
that way. JAY GOULD

How I Did It—215

I chose some people whose language was not English, and some who were Americans. I asked them to make a little cross next to anything that didn't sound right. If enough people marked a sentence, I knew something was wrong with it. JERZY KOSINSKI, on how
he learned to write in English

When I was young I used to go into the practice room and lock the door behind me. I'd put a beautiful novel in with my sheet music and a box of cherries on the right-hand side of the piano and a box of chocolates on the left and play runs with my left hand and eat cherries with my right and all the time be reading my book. ARTHUR RUBINSTEIN

Few people think more than two or three times a year; I have made an international reputation for myself by thinking once or twice a week. GEORGE BERNARD SHAW

Einstein once said that any man who liked marching had been given his brain for nothing; just the spinal column would have done. But I wasn't Einstein. Since most of one's time in the army is wasted anyway, I preferred to waste it by moving about in a precise manner. CLIVE JAMES

I have always tried to hide my efforts and wished my works to have the light joyousness

of springtime which never lets anyone suspect
the labors it has cost me.   HENRI MATISSE

> All the really good ideas I ever had came to
> me while I was milking a cow.
>   GRANT WOOD

All the inspiration I ever needed was a phone
call from a producer.   COLE PORTER

> I pretended to be somebody I wanted to be
> until I finally became that person. Or he be-
> came me.   CARY GRANT

I was a fourteen-year-old boy for thirty
years.   MICKEY ROONEY

> I knew if I continued to look around ... it
> would be difficult for me to contain my own
> emotions. So I turned away from the red eyes
> of the crowd and looked only at the red eye
> of the camera, talking to all the nation.
>   RICHARD NIXON, on his farewell
>   speech to the White House staff

I have learned throughout my life as a composer chiefly through my mistakes and pur-
suits of false assumptions, not by my exposure
to wisdom and founts of knowledge.
                              IGOR STRAVINSKY

People think that bullfights in my pictures were copied from life, but they are mistaken. I used to paint them before I'd seen the bullfight so as to make money to buy my ticket. PABLO PICASSO

I decided to become a genius.
DARRYL F. ZANUCK

I began wearing hats as a young lawyer because it helped me to establish my professional identity. Before that, whenever I was at a meeting, someone would ask me to get coffee—they assumed I was a secretary.

BELLA ABZUG

I got started dancing because I knew that was one way to meet girls.

GENE KELLY

I went into the business for the money, and the art grew out of it. If people are disillusioned by that remark, I can't help it. It's the truth.

CHARLIE CHAPLIN

I did it for the loot, honey, always the loot.

AVA GARDNER

I've done the most awful rubbish in order to have somewhere to go in the morning.

RICHARD BURTON

I didn't vant to be alone.

> HEDY LAMARR, on why
> she married five times

> It is true that I never should have married, but
> I didn't want to live without a man. Brought
> up to respect the conventions, love had to end
> in marriage. I'm afraid it did.   BETTE DAVIS

I never wanted to weigh more heavily on a
man than a bird.   COCO CHANEL, on why
> she never married

> I suppose one of the reasons why I grew up
> feeling the need to cause laughter was perpet-
> ual fear of being its unwitting object.

> CLIVE JAMES

You must realize that honorary degrees are
given generally to people whose SAT scores
were too low to get them into schools the regular way. As a matter of fact, it was my SAT
scores that led me into my present vocation in
life, comedy.   NEIL SIMON

> I was the originator, I was the emancipator, I
> was the architect of rock 'n' roll. And didn't
> nobody want to give me credit for it. I didn't

ask anybody for it because I just made it up and I didn't think—it's just like if you're barefoot and you make yourself a pair of shoes. When I made rock 'n' roll I got tired of the old people's music of that time. I did it because that's what I wanted to hear. I was tired of the slow music.   LITTLE RICHARD

I shaved my head because I was bored. You think a woman is aggressive just because she doesn't have any hair?   SINEAD O'CONNOR

I stopped making movies because I don't like taking my clothes off.   DEBBIE REYNOLDS

I was in the Victoria Library in Toronto in 1915, studying a Latin poet, and all of a sudden I thought, War can't be this bad. So I walked out and enlisted.   LESTER B. PEARSON

I have [converted to Roman Catholicism] because I want the discipline, the fire and the authority of the Church. I am hopelessly unworthy of it, but I hope to become worthy.
                    EDITH SITWELL

I've taken up the Bible again somewhat in the spirit of W. C. Fields—looking for loopholes.   DAVID NIVEN

I always wanted to blunt and blur what was painful. My idea [in taking drugs] was pain reduction and mind expansion, but I ended up with mind reduction and pain expansion.

CARRIE FISHER

I think I really wanted to write my biography more to be able to mention that Jack Kennedy and I were friends than anything else.

JERRY LEWIS

The banks couldn't afford me. That's why I had to be in business for myself.

SAMUEL GOLDWYN

I felt the urge to direct because I couldn't stomach what was being done with what I wrote.

JOSEPH L. MANKIEWICZ

I wasn't driven to acting by an inner compulsion. I was running away from the sporting goods business.

PAUL NEWMAN

I was never totally involved in movies. I was making my father's dream come true.

MARY ASTOR

I decided to become an actor because I was failing in school and I needed the credits.

DUSTIN HOFFMAN

When I was twelve years old my mother asked me to go to the store and buy some apples and warned me to pick good ones. But back then they came in baskets, not clear plastic containers. So I picked the best ones I could, brought them home and said, "Mom, look at these great apples." But only the ones on top were good; the rest were rotten. Thus was born a consumer advocate.   RALPH NADER

My main reason for adopting literature as a profession was that, as the author is never seen by his clients, he need not dress respectably.   GEORGE BERNARD SHAW

I played Little League baseball, and I was mediocrity under pressure. I played for the Mittendorf Funeral Home Panthers in Champaign, Illinois. The team's color was black, needless to say. I seem to recall playing second base, but I was a born right fielder, which is where they put the kid they can't figure out what to do with. As a hitter, I wanted to walk. I lacked athletic confidence, which is why I sank to journalism.   GEORGE WILL

Why did I write? Because I found life unsatisfactory.   TENNESSEE WILLIAMS

I've never made the film I wanted to make. No matter what happens, it never turns out exactly as I hoped. ROGER CORMAN

I made a lot of movies I wish I could turn into guitar picks. MARTIN LANDAU

I made all those musicals, comedies and adventure films, over all those years, but wherever I go, people only want to remember me for that one shower scene in *Psycho*. I feel like all these film historians are voyeurs, and I'm the constant object of their scrutinization. If I'd known thirty years ago that film students would be going over my body, frame by frame with a microscope, I probably would have asked for a body double. JANET LEIGH

Every man I knew had fallen in love with Gilda and wakened with me. RITA HAYWORTH

After *The Wizard of Oz* I was typecast as a lion, and there aren't all that many parts for lions. BERT LAHR

I made some mistakes in drama. I thought drama was when the actors cried. But drama is when the audience cries. FRANK CAPRA

I made the mistake early in my career, when I moved to Hollywood, of being attracted to actresses. I used to go out exclusively with actresses and all other female impersonators. MORT SAHL

One of my chief regrets during my years in the theater is that I couldn't sit in the audience and watch me. JOHN BARRYMORE

My major regret in life . . . is that my childhood was unnecessarily lonely. TRUMAN CAPOTE

I don't regret the rest of it at all, but I do regret the fact that I didn't stop to have a baby. STEVIE NICKS

I feel cheated never being able to know what it's like to get pregnant, carry a child and breast-feed. DUSTIN HOFFMAN

I always brought up my children not to believe in Mother's Day gifts, and now I regret it. LAUREN BACALL

I don't mind the celebrity status, and I don't mind signing autographs either. When I was a little girl, I missed getting Peggy Fleming's autograph, and I never forgot that.

DOROTHY HAMILL

I have only two regrets—that I have not shot Henry Clay or hanged John C. Calhoun.

ANDREW JACKSON

Worst damfool mistake I ever made was letting myself be elected Vice President of the United States. Should have stuck with my old chores as Speaker of the House. I gave up the second most important job in government for one that didn't amount to a hill of beans. I spent eight long years as Mr. Roosevelt's spare tire. I might still be speaker if I hadn't let them elect me vice president.

JOHN NANCE GARNER

I made one great mistake in my life—when I signed the letter to President Roosevelt recommending that atom bombs be made.

ALBERT EINSTEIN

The only thing I regret about my past is the length of it. If I had to live my life again I'd make the same mistakes, only sooner.

TALLULAH BANKHEAD

The one thing I regret is that I will never have time to read all the books I want to read.

FRANÇOISE SAGAN

I owned a tattoo parlor for a while. *Big* mistake. All of us got tattoos now, none of us want them. I got three of the fuckers. My wife has two. Even my Aunt Toots got a tattoo and she's fifty-seven.   JOHN COUGAR MELLENCAMP

I'd rather have written *Cheers* than anything I've written.   KURT VONNEGUT

The great sadness of my life is that I never achieved the hour newscast, which would not have been twice as good as the half-hour newscast, but many times as good.
   WALTER CRONKITE

As a kid, I dreamed of being a trapeze artist, but alas, I am not.   MARIEL HEMINGWAY

I always wanted to be some kind of writer or newspaper reporter. But after college . . . I did other things.   JACQUELINE ONASSIS

I really wanted to be an adventurer, to lay pipeline in South America or be a cabin boy . . . but I didn't have the guts.
   EDWARD ASNER

I have wasted my hours.   LEONARDO DA VINCI

I've over-educated myself in all the things I shouldn't have known.   NOEL COWARD

I don't know how it is that you start working at something that you don't like, and before you know it you're an old man.

HERMAN MANKIEWICZ

I was told that the Chinese said they would bury me by the Western Lake and build a shrine to my memory. I have some slight regret that this did not happen as I might have become a god, which would have been very chic for an atheist.

BERTRAND RUSSELL

I never gave anything away without wishing I had kept it, or kept it without wishing I had given it away.

LOUISE BROOKS

What I regret, on behalf of myself of long ago, is not the overweeningness, but the playing it safe.

ELIZABETH BOWEN

If I'd known I was gonna live this long I'd have taken better care of myself.

JIMMY DURANTE

I have no regrets. I wouldn't have lived my life the way I did if I was going to worry about what people were going to say.

INGRID BERGMAN

MOHANDAS K. GANDHI
The Shackles of Lust

The time of which I am now speaking is my sixteenth year. My father ... was bedridden, suffering from a fistula. My mother, an old servant of the house, and I were his principal attendants. I had the duties of a nurse, which mainly consisted in dressing the wound, giving my father his medicine, and compounding drugs whenever they had to be made up at home. Every night I massaged his legs and retired only when he asked me to do so or after he had fallen asleep. I loved to do this service. I do not remember ever having neglected it. All the time at my disposal, after the performance of the daily duties, was divided between school and attending on my father. I would only go out for an evening walk either when he permitted me or when he was feeling well.

This was also the time when my wife was expecting a baby,—a circumstance which, as I can see today, meant a double shame for me. For one thing I did not restrain myself, as I should have done, whilst I was yet a student. And secondly, this carnal lust got the better of what I regarded as my duty to study, and of what was even a greater duty, my devotion to my parents, Shravan having been my ideal since childhood. Every night whilst my hands were busy massaging my father's legs, my mind was hovering about the bed-room,—and that too at a time when religion, medical science and common sense alike forbade sexual intercourse. I was always glad to be relieved from my duty, and went straight to the bed-room after doing obeisance to my father.

At the same time my father was getting worse every day. Ayurvedic physicians had tried all their ointments, Hakims their plasters, and local quacks their nostrums. An English surgeon had also used his skill. As the last and only resort he had recommended a surgical operation. But the family physician came in the way. He disapproved of an operation being performed at such an advanced age. The physician was competent and well-known, and his advice prevailed. The operation was abandoned, and various medicines purchased for the purpose were of no account. I have an impression that if the physician had allowed the operation, the wound would have been easily healed. The operation also was to have been performed by a surgeon who was then well-known in Bombay. But God had willed otherwise. When death is imminent, who can think of the right remedy? My father returned from Bombay with all the paraphernalia of the operation, which were now useless. He despaired of living any longer. He was getting weaker and weaker, until at last he had to be asked to perform the necessary functions in bed. But up to the last he refused to do anything of the kind, always insisting on going through the strain of leaving his bed. The Vaishnavite rules about external cleanliness are so inexorable.

Such cleanliness is quite essential, no doubt, but Western medical science has taught us that all the functions, including a bath, can be done in bed with the strictest regard to cleanliness, and without the slightest discomfort to the patient, the bed always remaining spotlessly clean. I should regard such cleanliness as quite consistent with Vaishnavism. But my father's insistence on leaving the bed only struck me with wonder then, and I had nothing but admiration for it.

The dreadful night came. My uncle was then in Rajkot. I have a faint recollection that he came to Rajkot having had news that my father was getting worse. The brothers were deeply attached to each other. My uncle would sit near my father's bed the whole day, and would insist on sleeping by his bed-side after sending us all to sleep. No one had dreamt that this was to be the fateful night. The danger of course was there.

It was 10:30 or 11:00 P.M. I was giving the massage. My uncle offered to relieve me. I was glad and went straight to the bed-room. My wife, poor thing, was fast asleep. But how could she sleep when I was there? I woke her up. In five or six minutes, however, the servant knocked at the door. I started with alarm. "Get up," he said, "Father is very ill." I knew of course that he was very ill, and so I guessed what "very ill" meant at that moment. I sprang out of bed.

"What is the matter? Do tell me!"

"Father is no more."

So all was over! I had but to wring my hands. I felt deeply ashamed and miserable. I ran to my father's room, I saw that if animal passion had not blinded me, I should have been spared the torture of separation from my father during his last moments. I should have been massaging him, and he would have died in my arms. But now it was my uncle who had had this privilege. He was so deeply devoted to his elder brother that he had earned the honor of doing him the last services! My father had had forebodings of the coming event. He had made a sign for pen and paper, and written: "Prepare for the last rites." He had then snapped the amulet off his arm and also his gold necklace of *tulasi*-beads and flung them aside. A moment after this he was no more. . . .

This shame of my carnal desire even at the critical hour of my father's death . . . is a blot I have never been able to efface or forget, and I have always thought that although my devotion to my parents knew no bounds and I would have given up anything for it, yet it was weighed and found unpardonably wanting because my mind was at the same moment in the grip of lust. I have therefore always regarded myself as a lustful, though a faithful, husband. It took me long to get free from the shackles of lust, and I had to pass through many ordeals before I could overcome it.

Before I close this chapter of my double shame, I may mention that the poor mite that was born to my wife scarcely breathed for more than three or four days. Nothing else could be expected. Let all those who are married be warned by my example.

Where I Stand

I don't hate homosexuals. I love homosexuals.
It's the sin of homosexuality I hate.

ANITA BRYANT

I'm not against the blacks, and a lot of the good
blacks will attest to that.　　EVAN MECHAM

I hate all earthlings.　JAMES DEAN

I cannot and will not cut my conscience to
suit this year's fashions.　　LILLIAN HELLMAN

I detest bad manners. If people are polite, then
I am; they shouldn't try to get away with not
being polite to me.　　FRANK SINATRA

I passionately hate the idea of being "with it."
I think an artist is always out of step with his
time. He has to be.　　ORSON WELLES

I do not like broccoli and I haven't liked it since I was a little kid and my mother made me eat it. And I'm President of the United States, and I'm not going to eat any more broccoli.

GEORGE BUSH

In social affairs, I'm an optimist. I really do believe that our military-industrial civilization will soon collapse.   EDWARD ABBEY

The only person I really believe in is me.
DEBORAH HARRY

I know myself too well to believe in pure virtue.   ALBERT CAMUS

While there is a lower class, I am in it; while there is a criminal element, I am of it; while there is a soul in prison, I am not free.
EUGENE V. DEBS

My philosophy is that I can be unhappy for a little period of time, but I don't like to feel unhappiness for long periods of time.
GOLDIE HAWN

I think nudity on the stage is disgusting, shameful and unpatriotic. But if I were twenty-two with a great body, it would be artistic, tasteful, patriotic and a progressive, religious experience.   SHELLEY WINTERS

To me, bad taste is what entertainment is all about.   JOHN WATERS

On matters of intonation and technicalities, I am more than a martinet—I am a martinetissimo.   LEOPOLD STOKOWSKI

I just don't think women should be in an orchestra. They become men. Men treat them as equals; they even change their pants in front of them. I think it is terrible.　ZUBIN MEHTA

I do not believe in using women in combat, because females are too fierce.

　　　　　　　　　　MARGARET MEAD

I'm a vegetarian. I don't know why.

　　　　　　　　　　STEVE MARTIN

I'm not a vegetarian because I love animals; I'm a vegetarian because I hate plants.

　　　　　　　A. WHITNEY BROWN

I believe that mink are raised for being turned into fur coats and if we didn't wear fur coats those little animals would never have been born. So is it better not to have been born or to have lived for a year or two to have been turned into a fur coat? I don't know.

　　　　　　　　　　BARBIE BENTON

A Chicken McNugget doesn't die any easier than baby fur seals, and the fact that somebody could be so insipid to think that the chicken has less rights than the baby fur seal because it's not as cute can kiss my ass.

　　　　　　　　　　TED NUGENT

I'm in favor of animal liberation. Why? Because I'm an animal. EDWARD ABBEY

I believe in my family; nothing comes before them. I believe in being outraged by violations of human rights. I believe in using words, not fists. I believe in my outrage knowing people are living in boxes on the street. I believe we need to start listening to people in this country. I believe in honesty. I believe in a good time. I believe in good food. I believe in sex. SUSAN SARANDON

Basically, I believe the world is a jungle, and if it's not a bit of a jungle in the home, a child cannot possibly be fit to enter the outside world. BETTE DAVIS

I think husbands and wives should live in separate houses. If there's enough money, the children should live in a third. CLORIS LEACHMAN

When I hear an actress say, "You know what, I'm gonna have my face done, get my tits raised, and I'm going to get another ten years out of this business," I say, "More power to you. Go do it." MICHELLE PFEIFFER

I am a man of fixed and unbending principles, the first of which is to be flexible at all times. EVERETT DIRKSEN

I don't like principles. I prefer prejudices.

OSCAR WILDE

I think greed is healthy. You can be greedy
and still feel good about yourself.

IVAN BOESKY

At one point you have to say, "Am I an American, or am I a journalist?" The fact is, I am
an American journalist. DAN RATHER

I'm for bringing back the birch. But only between consenting adults. GORE VIDAL

I believe capital punishment to be an appropriate remedy for anyone who does me injury,
but under no other circumstances.

F. LEE BAILEY

I would die for my country but I could never
let my country die for me. NEIL KINNOCK

I'll go through life either first class or third,
but never in second. NOEL COWARD

Anything that won't sell, I don't want to
invent. THOMAS A. EDISON

People are much too solemn about things—I'm
all for sticking pins into episcopal behinds. ALDOUS HUXLEY

As far as I'm concerned, there won't be a
Beatles reunion as long as John Lennon remains dead.　　　　　　GEORGE HARRISON

> I would rather be an opportunist and float than
> go to the bottom with my principles round my
> neck.　　　　　　STANLEY BALDWIN

I'm a dyed-in-the-wool party man. I don't
know just what party I am in right now, but I
am for the party.　　HUEY "KINGFISH" LONG

> I'll speak for the man, or against him, which-
> ever will do the most good.　RICHARD NIXON

I'm about as left-wing as it's possible to go.
　　　　　　　　VANESSA REDGRAVE

> My political opinions lean more and more to-
> ward anarchy.　　　　　J.R.R. TOLKIEN

I am a Tory Anarchist. I should like everyone
to go about doing just as he pleased—short of
altering any of the things to which I have
grown accustomed.　　　MAX BEERBOHM

> I'm a registered Republican and consider so-
> cialism a violation of the American principle
> that you shouldn't stick your nose in other
> people's business except to make a buck.
> 　　　　　　　　P. J. O'ROURKE

I'm a card-carrying member of the A.C.L.U.
and the N.R.A.   DAVID MAMET

> I'm not a member of any establishment. I'm
> too intuitional for the intellectuals and too
> conservative for the way-out. EDWARD ALBEE

I used to believe that anything was better than
nothing. Now I know that sometimes nothing
is better.   GLENDA JACKSON

> I'm frankly a bourgeois living in seclusion in
> the country, busy with literature and asking
> nothing of anyone, not consideration, or
> honor, or esteem. . . . I'd jump into the water
> to save a good line of poetry or a good sen-
> tence of prose from anyone. But I don't be-
> lieve, on that account, that humanity has need
> of me, any more than I have need of it.
>   GUSTAVE FLAUBERT

I don't believe in that "no comment" business.
I always have a comment. MARTHA MITCHELL

> In the depths of my heart I can't help being
> convinced that my dear fellow men, with a
> few exceptions, are worthless.
>   SIGMUND FREUD

I don't love humanity. I don't hate them either.
I just don't know them personally.
                              ALAN ARKIN

I do not believe . . . I know.   CARL JUNG

I hate the idea of causes, and if I had to choose
between betraying my country and betraying
my friend, I hope I should have the guts to
betray my country.   E. M. FORSTER

I think a man ought to get drunk at least twice
a year just on principle, so he won't let himself
get snotty about it.   RAYMOND CHANDLER

I don't want anybody calling me Ms.
                ANN LANDERS

To me the expression Ms. really means
misery.   PHYLLIS SCHLAFLY

I have nothing against gays or lesbians. I have
lots of gay boys working for me.
                ZSA ZSA GABOR

My attitude toward men who mess around is
simple: If you find 'em, kill 'em.
                LORETTA LYNN

If I'm going to hell, I'm going there playing the
piano.   JERRY LEE LEWIS

I won't buy a magazine that would publish
what I write.   GOODMAN ACE

I'll balance a dog biscuit on my nose if it causes enough people to tune us in. TED KOPPEL

I respect kindness to human beings first of all, and kindness to animals. I don't respect the law; I have a total irreverence for anything connected with society, except that which makes the roads safer, the beer stronger, the food cheaper, and old men and old women warmer in the winter and happier in the summer. BRENDAN BEHAN

I am probably the only living American, black or white, who just doesn't give a damn. ADAM CLAYTON POWELL

I should have the courage of my lack of convictions. TOM STOPPARD

I'm not a suicide freak, but I want to be free. If I ever have a terminal disease that would affect my mind or my body, I would end it. JERZY KOSINSKI

I have nothing against undertakers personally. It's just that I wouldn't want one to bury my sister. JESSICA MITFORD

I have nothing to say and I am saying it. JOHN CAGE

I am an Anglo-Catholic in religion, a classicist in literature and a royalist in politics.

T. S. ELIOT

I'm an Irish Catholic and I have a long iceberg of guilt.

EDNA O'BRIEN

I'm a Communist by day and a Catholic as soon as it gets dark.

BRENDAN BEHAN

I'm one of those cliff-hanging Catholics. I don't believe in God, but I do believe that Mary was his mother.

MARTIN SHEEN

I was an atheist. Then I became a Christian. Then I became a born-again Christian, and now I have become a Christian patriot. And all that happened in a two-week period.

LARRY FLYNT

I want nothing to do with any religion concerned with keeping the masses satisfied to live in hunger, filth and ignorance. I want nothing to do with any order, religious or otherwise, which does not teach people that they are capable of becoming happier and more civilized.   JAWAHARLAL NEHRU

I am a temporary enclosure for a temporary purpose; that served, my skull and teeth, my idiosyncrasy and desire, will disperse, I believe, like the timbers of a booth after a fair.   H. G. WELLS

I am prepared to meet my Maker. Whether my Maker is prepared for the great ordeal of meeting me is another matter.
                          WINSTON CHURCHILL

I respect faith, but doubt is what gets you an education.   WILSON MIZNER

I believe in God because I have lost my faith in reason and the progress of thought.
                          BEN HECHT

I could prove God statistically.
                          GEORGE GALLUP

I don't believe in God, but I do believe in his saints.   EDITH WHARTON

I believe in God, only I spell it Nature.

FRANK LLOYD WRIGHT

I believe in Original Sin. I find people profoundly bad and irresistibly funny.

JOE ORTON

I believe the wrong God is temporarily running the world and that the true God has gone under. ANTHONY BURGESS

I do benefits for all religions; I don't want to blow the hereafter on a technicality.

BOB HOPE

Thank God, I am still an atheist.

LUIS BUÑUEL

I never said, "I want to be alone." I only said, "I want to be let alone."   GRETA GARBO

Some people claim I say all actors are cattle. What I say is all actors should be *treated* like cattle.   ALFRED HITCHCOCK

I'm not a Jew. I'm Jew-*ish*. I don't go the whole hog.   JONATHAN MILLER

If I take refuge in ambiguity, I assure you that it's quite conscious.   KINGMAN BREWSTER, JR.

I never wanted to be famous; I only wanted to be great.   RAY CHARLES

I don't want loyalty. I want *loyalty*.
LYNDON BAINES JOHNSON

To betray, you must first belong. I never belonged. KIM PHILBY

I was beastly but never coarse. A high-class sort of heel. GEORGE SANDERS

Hell, if I'd jumped on all the dames I'm supposed to have jumped on, I'd have had no time to go fishing. CLARK GABLE

Everybody makes me out to be some kind of macho pig, humping women in the gutter. I do, but I put a pillow under them first. JAMES CAAN

I was always an independent, even when I had partners. SAMUEL GOLDWYN

I'm not really Henry Fonda. Nobody could have that much integrity. HENRY FONDA

I'm not a rock star. SINEAD O'CONNOR

I am not a crook. RICHARD NIXON

I'm a Ford, not a Lincoln. GERALD FORD

I'm not a stunt man. I'm not a daredevil. I'm an explorer. EVEL KNIEVEL

I am not a lesbian and I am not a slut.
VANESSA WILLIAMS

I am like any other man. All I do is supply a
demand. AL CAPONE

I have taken more out of alcohol than alcohol
has taken out of me. WINSTON CHURCHILL

I'm no alcoholic. I'm a drunkard. The difference is, drunkards don't go to meetings.
JACKIE GLEASON

I am only a beer teetotaler, not a champagne
teetotaler. GEORGE BERNARD SHAW

I don't mind a little praise—as long as it's
fulsome. ADLAI STEVENSON

I didn't invent the world I write about—it's all
true. GRAHAM GREENE

I am not a great man. I have made a great
discovery. SIGMUND FREUD

I don't write modern music. I only write good
music. IGOR STRAVINSKY

I can't say I was ever lost, but I was bewildered
once for three days. DANIEL BOONE

I take a lot of crap, a lot of insults, a lot of
humiliation. Some of it's self-generated and
some of it promulgated by people who see
only this neolithic, primordial image. I'm not
a right-wing jingoistic human being. Rambo is.
He's psychotic. In many ways.

SYLVESTER STALLONE

I am patient with stupidity, but not with those
who are proud of it.   EDITH SITWELL

I do not mind lying, but I hate inaccuracy.

SAMUEL BUTLER

I don't want you to think I'm not in-
coherent.   HAROLD ROSS

I don't mean I'm really going mad, but I'm a
little crazy.   GENA ROWLANDS

I adore life but I don't fear death. I just prefer
to die as late as possible.   GEORGES SIMENON

I didn't kill anyone that didn't deserve killing
in the first place.   MICKEY COHEN

I've never been poor, only broke. Being poor
is a frame of mind. Being broke is only a temporary situation.   MIKE TODD

I'm cheerful, I'm not happy. There's a big difference.   BEVERLY SILLS

You know, all that stuff I call men—"hot slabs of meat," "love slaves," "pigs"—that's all affectionate.   JUDY TENUTA

I dress for women, and undress for men.
      ANGIE DICKINSON

I've always been behind musically but ahead politically.   JOAN BAEZ

I'm not a snob. Ask anybody. Well, anybody who matters.   SIMON LE BON

[Having a sensitive-guy image] is a real pain in the ass. In fact, I have a very colorful vocabulary.   ALAN ALDA

I have my standards. They may be low, but I have them.   BETTE MIDLER

I neither was nor am holier than thou. I've seen about everything, heard just about everything and done part of it.
      SENATOR JESSE HELMS

It's not true that I had nothing on. I had the radio on.   MARILYN MONROE, on posing nude for a calendar

I was naughty. I wasn't bad. Bad is hurting
people, doing evil. Naughty is being
amusing.   SYDNEY BIDDLE BARROWS

> It is not my mode of thought that has caused
> my misfortunes, but the mode of thought of
> others.   MARQUIS DE SADE

I'm a student of violence because I'm a student
of the human heart.   SAM PECKINPAH

> The only difference between me and my fel-
> low actors is that I've spent more time in
> jail.   ROBERT MITCHUM

I'm not Vic Virile.   TOM SELLECK

> I'm not the Carter who'll never tell a lie.
>   BILLY CARTER

I'm not a speed reader. I'm a speed under-
stander.   ISAAC ASIMOV

> I've always been interested in people, but I've
> never liked them.   W. SOMERSET MAUGHAM

I love mankind; it's people I can't stand.
                            CHARLES SCHULTZ

I never wanted to be a millionaire. I just wanted to live like one.   WALTER HAGEN

I am not rich. I am a poor man with money, which is not the same thing.

GABRIEL GARCÍA MÁRQUEZ

I won't say my previous husbands thought only of my money, but it had a certain fascination for them.   BARBARA HUTTON

Don't get the idea that I'm one of these god-damn radicals. Don't get the idea that I'm knocking the American system.   AL CAPONE

I am an American and I have lived half my life in Paris, not the half which made me, but the half in which I made what I made.

GERTRUDE STEIN

The famous soft watches are nothing else than the tender, extravagant, solitary, paranoiac-critical camembert of time and space.

SALVADOR DALI

The things that I have apparently parodied I actually admire.   ROY LICHTENSTEIN

If I would be in this business for *business*, I wouldn't be in this business.   SOL HUROK

The hair is real; it's the head that's fake.

STEVE ALLEN

I am sufficiently proud of my knowing something to be modest about my not knowing everything. VLADIMIR NABOKOV

I can't say, over the miles, that I had learned what I had wanted to know because I hadn't known what I wanted to know. But I *did* learn what I didn't know I wanted to know.

WILLIAM LEAST HEAT MOON

I may not know much, but I know chicken shit from chicken salad. LYNDON BAINES JOHNSON

I am always ready to learn although I do not always like being taught.

WINSTON CHURCHILL

It's not the most intellectual job in the world, but I do have to know the letters.

VANNA WHITE

[We were] two persons who never argued over anything except the use of a subjunctive.

JEAN HARRIS of her relationship
with Dr. Herman Tarnower

We never claimed that we walked on water. YOKO ONO

Somebody said to me, "But the Beatles were anti-materialistic." That's a huge myth. John and I literally used to sit down and say, "Now, let's write a swimming pool." PAUL McCARTNEY

Nothing I have said is factual except the bits that sound like fiction. CLIVE JAMES (in his autobiography)

It was a mixed marriage. I'm human, he was a Klingon. CAROL LEIFER

I never set out to be weird. It was always other people who called me weird. FRANK ZAPPA

I'm a nut, but not just a nut. BILL MURRAY

I'm not confused, I'm just well mixed. ROBERT FROST

I say I don't sleep with married men, but what I mean is that I don't sleep with happily married men. BRITT EKLAND

No matter which sex I went to bed with, I never smoked on the street. FLORENCE KING

There really isn't a Steve Lawrence, you know.
Eydie's a ventriloquist.   STEVE LAWRENCE

I am not a dog-lover. To me, a dog-lover is a
dog who is in love with another dog.
                              JAMES THURBER

God makes stars; I just produce them.
                              SAMUEL GOLDWYN

I am not a product of privilege, I am a product
of opportunity.   EDWARD HEATH

I'm not an agent. I'm an engineer of
careers.   MARK McCORMACK

I am not a glutton—I am an explorer of
food.   ERMA BOMBECK

I really didn't say everything I said.
                              YOGI BERRA

MADONNA
Our Lady of Perpetual Confession

PART IV

I wanted to be a big star. I wanted to dance. I wanted to sing. I wanted to be famous, I wanted everybody to love me.

I became an overachiever to get approval from the world.

I don't want to be the world's greatest singer or dancer; I want to push people's buttons, I want to be provocative, I want to be political.

I don't believe in gratuitous violence and I don't believe in degradation of any human being. . . . And I would never promote those things in any of my art, and I don't.

I'm a vegetarian. I used not to eat anything that could take a shit. Now I eat fish. I changed it to not eating anything that walks on the earth.

There's a lot of stuff [in the movie, *Truth or Dare*] with Warren [Beatty] that

I'm a political person. It excites me to be a political person. . . . But I want to have fun while I'm doing it.   MADONNA

I cut out—there were phone conversations I thought were really moving and touching and revealing, but Warren didn't know we were recording it. It wasn't fair, plus it's a federal offense.

I'm terrified of cockroaches. I can't even look at them. Whenever I saw them in my cupboard in New York, I screamed and ran away.

I have an iron will. And all of my will has always been to conquer some horrible feeling of inadequacy. I'm always struggling with that fear. I push past one spell of it and discover myself as a special human being, and then I get to another stage and think I'm mediocre and uninteresting. And I find a way to get myself out of that. Again and again. My drive in life is from this horrible fear of being mediocre. And that's always pushing me, pushing me. Because even though I've become Somebody, I still have to prove that I'm *Somebody*. My struggle has never ended and it probably never will.

Sitting on the toilet peeing—that's where I have my most contemplative moments.

How could I have been anything else but what I am, having been named Madonna? I would either have ended up a nun or this.

I missed being an elevator boy by about that much, when my mother reached up and made me go back to school after laying out for two years. LYNDON BAINES JOHNSON

I didn't go to high school and I didn't go to grade school, either. Education, I think, is for refinement and is probably a liability.

H. L. HUNT

My mother has always been unhappy with what I do. She would much rather I do something nicer, like be a bricklayer. MICK JAGGER

I went to this party in the sixties and saw this beautiful woman in a see-through yellow blouse with nothing underneath. I kept staring at her, but when she said, "Why don't you come home with me?" I ran out the door. Twenty-five years later I found out who the woman was: Greta Garbo. BURT REYNOLDS

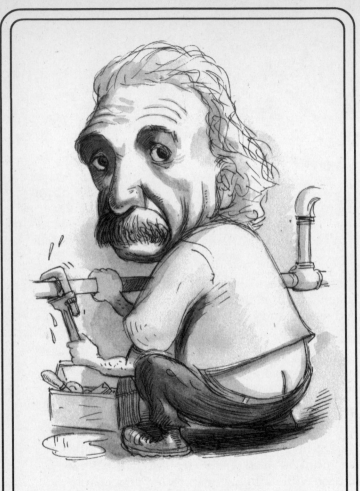

If I had my life to live over again, I'd be a plumber.   ALBERT EINSTEIN

I have often thought that if there had been a good rap group around in those days, I might have chosen a career in music instead of politics.   RICHARD NIXON

I was seventeen and making *Shampoo* [when Warren Beatty] offered to relieve me of the huge burden of my virginity. Four times. That was the big offer. I decided against it. I decided for reality over anecdote.
                        CARRIE FISHER

When Ava [Gardner] got divorced she called me and told me I could marry her, but it was too late. The truth is I couldn't have gone on with her. She didn't leave me any time for my bulls.   LUIS MIGUEL DOMINGUÍN

You have no idea of the people I *didn't* marry.   ARTIE SHAW

I always wanted to be a writer, but I became an actor because we were very poor and I had an uncle in show business who was making $200 a week, and I wasn't making anything, not even an occasional girl.   GROUCHO MARX

If I had learned to type, I never would have made brigadier general.
                        BRIGADIER GENERAL
                        ELIZABETH P. HOISINGTON,
                        U.S. Army

If I hadn't been a star I would have been a beautician or a missionary.   DOLLY PARTON

I could have made a fortune as a dominatrix.   CAMILLE PAGLIA

If my books had been any worse I would not have been invited to Hollywood, and if they had been any better I would not have come.   RAYMOND CHANDLER

Though I've lived in the rural West most of my life, I never once fell in love with a horse. Not once. Neither end.   EDWARD ABBEY

Summing Up

I've had an exciting life. I married for love and got a little money along with it.

ROSE KENNEDY

In three words I can sum up everything I've learned about life. It goes on.   ROBERT FROST

For me, life has been either a wake or a wedding.   PETER O'TOOLE

I did it *my way*.   PAUL ANKA

I never hurt nobody but myself and that's nobody's business but my own.   BILLIE HOLIDAY

I have never seasoned a truth with the sauce of a lie in order to digest it more easily.

MARGUERITE YOURCENAR

I have been taking stock of my fifty years since I left Wichita in 1922 at the age of fifteen to become a dancer. . . . How I have existed fills me with horror. For I failed in everything—spelling, arithmetic, riding, swimming, tennis, golf, dancing, singing, acting, wife, mistress, whore, friend. Even cooking. And I do not excuse myself with the usual escape of "not trying." I tried with all my heart.

LOUISE BROOKS

Everyone tells me I've had such an interesting life, but sometimes I think it's been nothing but stomach disturbances and self-concern. CARY GRANT

I have a child and I have made a few people happy. That is all. MARLENE DIETRICH

I've had a hell of a lot of fun, and I've enjoyed every minute of it. ERROL FLYNN

I started at the top and worked down.

ORSON WELLES

I haven't had everything from life, I've had too much. RITA HAYWORTH

When I was young, there was Saran Wrap. Now there's fax. I feel I've seen everything. GORE VIDAL

To sum it all up, I must say that I regret
nothing.   ADOLF EICHMANN

I have been very happy, very rich, very beautiful, much adulated, very famous and very
unhappy.   BRIGITTE BARDOT

I was much too far out all my life. And not
waving but drowning.   STEVIE SMITH

I was lucky, you know. I always had a beautiful girl and the money was good. Although I
would have done the whole thing over for, oh,
perhaps half.   BOB HOPE

I have always disliked myself at any given moment; the total of such moments is my life.
                            CYRIL CONNOLLY

I never really thought I'd make the grade. And
let's face it, I haven't.   GEORGE SANDERS

I always thought if you worked hard enough
and tried hard enough, things would work out.
I was wrong.   KATHERINE GRAHAM

When I was young, I used to think that wealth
and power would bring me happiness. I was
right.   GAHAN WILSON

In some situations I was difficult, in odd moments impossible, in rare moments loathsome, but at my best unapproachably great.

OSCAR LEVANT

If I had my life to live over again, I would have a different father, a different wife and a different religion.   JOHN F. KENNEDY

If I had my career over again? Maybe I'd say to myself, speed it up a little.

JAMES STEWART

My life is composed of random, tangential disparate episodes. Five wives: many liaisons, some more memorable than the marriages. The hunting. The betting. The thoroughbreds. Painting, collecting, boxing. Writing, directing and acting in more than sixty pictures.

JOHN HUSTON

I have sacrificed everything in my life that I consider precious in order to advance the political career of my husband.   PAT NIXON

One of the few lessons I have learned in life is that there is invariably something odd about women who wear ankle socks.

ALAN BENNETT

Life was so good to me. I had a great wife,
good kids, money, my own health—and I'm
lonely and bored.   O. J. Simpson

I was born in 1947. I have a wife, a child, a
mortgage, two dogs and gum disease.
                            Dave Barry

There comes a time in every man's life and
I've had many of them.   Casey Stengel

My Own Epitaph

He was an average guy who could carry a tune.　BING CROSBY

Excuse my dust.　DOROTHY PARKER

On the whole, I'd rather be in Philadelphia.
　W. C. FIELDS

Here lies one whose name was writ in water.　JOHN KEATS

If, after I depart this vale, you ever remember me and have thought to please my ghost, forgive some sinner and wink your eye at some homely girl.　H. L. MENCKEN

I'll be right back.　JOHNNY CARSON

I would die happy if I knew that on my tombstone could be written these words, "This man

was an absolute fool. None of the disastrous
things that he reluctantly predicted ever came
to pass!"   LEWIS MUMFORD

I always thought I'd like my own tombstone
to be blank. No epitaph, and no name. Well,
actually, I'd like it to say "figment."
                                 ANDY WARHOL

She did it the hard way.   BETTE DAVIS

Here lies Paul Newman, who died a failure
because his eyes turned brown.
                                 PAUL NEWMAN

Here lies Vincente Minnelli. He died of hard
work.   VINCENTE MINNELLI

He made the books and he died.
                                 WILLIAM FAULKNER

I had a lover's quarrel with the world.
                                 ROBERT FROST

When I am dead and buried, on my tombstone
I would like to have it written, "I have arrived." Because when you feel that you have
arrived, you are dead.   YUL BRYNNER

I never liked it anyhow. CHARLES BUKOWSKI

I died laughing. PHYLLIS DILLER

Since I am already eighty-two years old and see no end in sight, it might be appropriate to write, "And about time." QUENTIN CRISP

He never missed a deadline. HERB CAEN

He finally met a deadline. LARRY L. KING

He put on a good show. WILLIE NELSON

He had too much class for the room.
DAN GREENBURG

Know changes
Have Tux
Will Travel
    DAVE BRUBECK

He showed pretty good control for a south-paw. ELMORE LEONARD

I'll be seeing you shortly. FRED DeCORDOVA

It's *always* a beautiful day in this neigh-borhood. FRED ROGERS

Here lies David Zucker, as always, surrounded
by incompetence.   DAVID ZUCKER

[. . . pause] DAVID MAMET

This is one trial I wish I could have
avoided.   WILLIAM KUNSTLER

I've played everything but a harp.
                              LIONEL BARRYMORE

Over my dead body! GEORGE S. KAUFMAN

The guys with the lettuce get all the to-
matoes.   OLEG CASSINI

He found out the secret was to have fun.
                              ORSON BEAN

Surely there must be better gifts God could
have given us than life.
                          MICHAEL O'DONOGHUE

He finished the long trek alone.
                              ANTHONY QUINN

Let's do lunch next week.
                          RAOUL LIONEL FELDER

At last, time to catch up on my reading.
W. P. KINSELLA

Go Dawgs   LEWIS GRIZZARD

Maid: Please Make Up Room
CHRISTOPHER BUCKLEY

Uneven   LORNE MICHAELS

What are you looking at?   IAN SHOALES